BBC GoodFood
Vegetarian Food
for Friends

About the Author

Mary Gwynn trained at Leith's School of Food and Wine in London. From there she went to the *Good Housekeeping* Institute and spent two years working as a home economist on the magazine's food pages.

After a period travelling and working in the Far and Middle East she returned to London and became the Deputy Cookery Editor of *Woman and Home*, leaving after four years to work as a freelance home economist and food writer whilst her two daughters were young.

Mary has been Editor of *BBC Vegetarian Good Food* magazine since it was launched in spring 1992. Originally a quarterly magazine, it proved so popular that it is now issued every month.

Mary Gwynn regularly talks on local radio and gives cookery demonstrations at shows such as *BBC Good Food* Cooking and Kitchen Show and *Gardeners' World* Live.

Vegetarian Food for Friends

OVER 150 NEW VEGETARIAN RECIPES

Mary Gwynn

Photographs by Gus Filgate

BBC BOOKS

Acknowledgements

This book has been a pleasure to work on from start to finish thanks to the help and encouragement I've had from family and colleagues. In particular my thanks go to Heather Holden-Brown and Nicky Copeland at BBC Books for their support, and to Jane Middleton for her efficient and thorough editing. While writing the book, the team of Gus Filgate and Louise Pickford as photographer and home economist was always in mind – luckily the designer had the same idea and as a result the recipes have been brought vividly to life in stunning photographs throughout the book.

On the home front, thanks are due to my sister-in-law Debbie Butler for testing the recipes so patiently, to my husband Mark for all his tireless support as a single parent during the months I was either in the kitchen or at the computer, to my mother for being at the other end of the phone, and finally to Lucy and Isobel for trying almost everything I put in front of them and not complaining.

Published by BBC Books,
an imprint of BBC Worldwide Publishing.
BBC Worldwide Limited, Woodlands,
80 Wood Lane, London W12 0TT

First published 1995
© Mary Gwynn 1995
The moral right of the author has been asserted

ISBN 0 563 37105 6

Photographs by Gus Filgate
Styling by Penny Markham
Home Economist Louise Pickford
Illustrations by Sue Windett

Set in Caslon
Printed in Great Britain by Cambus Litho Ltd, East Kilbride
Bound in Great Britain by Hunter & Foulis Ltd, Edinburgh
Colour separations by Radstock Reproductions, Midsomer Norton
Cover printed by Clays Ltd, St Ives plc

Contents

Introduction

$\mathcal{W}$HEN I FIRST STARTED to plan this book, at a time when new vegetarian cookery books seemed to be appearing at a rate of knots, a friend asked me why I wanted to produce yet another volume of recipes. What, she wondered, would make mine any different from the others. This set me thinking. Like most keen cooks I have a collection of much-thumbed, oil-splattered recipe books in my kitchen, often with the most-used pages stuck back in with sticky tape. These sit amongst many other cookbooks which occasionally get taken down, glanced through and put straight back on the shelf. What is it that sets the former apart from the latter? Whatever it was, I had yet to find a vegetarian book that fitted into the grease-stained category.

Food, and the wonderful feeling of well-being that comes from sharing a meal with like-minded people, has always been one of the greatest pleasures of my life. I come from a family whose main form of celebrating any event is to sit round a table enjoying the twin delights of good company and good food. When I was a child we regularly ate out for special events such as birthdays, but Sundays always meant at least ten people round the dining-room table for lunch. My father travelled a lot in connection with his work and there were often foreign guests, family friends, including mine and my sisters' from school and later university – in fact anyone who happened to have had contact with the family in the preceding week. Numbers seemed endlessly flexible, as was the amount of food served. My mother just laid another place and one of us prepared some extra vegetables to cope with additions.

Though it would be wrong to say that the food we ate at such times was unimportant, there was never an enormous fuss made about it – it was simply a means of bringing people together. And I think that this point has a great deal of relevance for me still and the way I cook, and was fundamental in my desire to write this book. Cooking for other people should be a pleasure for everyone involved, and worry about its preparation or the way it is served should never overwhelm enjoyment of the occasion.

Unfortunately this is not always the case for some of us, especially when it comes to vegetarian cooking. Many people feel somehow threatened by the prospect of entertaining a vegetarian. Yet cooking without meat or fish is just another style of preparing food, in many ways rather like Chinese, Italian or low-fat cuisine – most people eat it at some time, some more regularly than others. I firmly believe that creating different dishes for individual guests takes all the pleasure out of preparing a meal and makes the visitor with special requirements feel very uncomfortable. Surely it's easier by far to plan one menu that will suit everyone. This is what I wanted this book to be about – a cookbook that brought people together with recipes that everyone, including the cook, would enjoy.

Creating a balanced and interesting vegetarian menu is the initial challenge to overcome, and I think that to do it well we need to move away from the idea of a focal dish that is served in the middle of the meal. One of the joys of travel is discovering how different nations prepare their vegetable produce, and it's to the advantage of everyone, vegetarian or carnivore, that the way we cook is now being influenced by cuisines as varied as Thai, North African and regional Indian. Whether for religious or economic reasons, many of these, especially the thrifty peasant styles of cooking, are almost totally vegetarian, and we can learn a lot from them when it comes to planning a menu. There is no point in trying to find a vegetarian alternative for leg of lamb and serving it as if it were meat; your meal will simply seem like a dull imitation. Look at the meal as a whole – just think of any Asian meal where a selection of dishes are served together to make an overall impact. I like to serve a trio of contrasting starters, for example, followed by a simple dish of pasta and finally a spectacular dessert. Pay a lot of attention to colour, texture and flavour; try to make sure everything isn't brown or green, and don't serve all bland or all spicy dishes together.

I do appreciate that for many people a meal is not complete without meat, and so in keeping with my aim to make life as easy as possible for the cook, some recipes in this book have tips on how to incorporate meat or fish in them. However, I would like to point out that all the recipes were created to stand alone without these additions, and I've only made suggestions that I think really work.

I hope I have managed to create a practical recipe book that doesn't treat vegetarians as a race apart and will appeal to anyone who enjoys cooking and eating, whatever their dietary persuasion. Let's follow the example of the many countries influencing the way we eat today by allowing vegetables to emerge from the sidelines and take centre stage in our meals. By doing so we are not only widening our culinary horizons but also improving our diets. What could be better?

Notes on the Recipes

1. Use either metric or imperial measurements throughout the recipes.

2. All eggs used are size three unless otherwise stated. I suggest you look out for free range eggs from a reputable local source.

3. Spoon measurements are all level unless otherwise stated.

4. I usually use a supermarket extra virgin olive oil for general recipes; you can use a milder olive oil if you prefer. When I specify extra virgin oil in a recipe I would recommend an estate-bottled oil for its stronger more intense flavour. This is the oil that I always use in salad dressings. For Asian style dishes I use sunflower or grapeseed oil.

5. Strict vegetarians should check that the cheeses they cook with are not made with animal rennet. Most commercial cheeses are now made with a non-animal rennet but are not always labelled so. Check with the manufacturer if you are unsure.

Soups

Soups are a favourite of mine for their enormous versatility and ease of preparation. Home-made soups taste immeasurably better than bought ones and make perfect comfort food. A hearty soup can be served as a main course, especially if it contains pulses; simply accompany it with good bread and a colourful salad, follow up with fresh fruit and cheese and you have a healthy, nutritious and delicious meal that is ideal for a casual get-together. First-course soups are usually more delicate and shouldn't be too filling. All soups rely on good stock (see page 186) for flavour, so don't cut corners on this if you can help it. I try to make stock once a month, then boil it down to a reduction which I store in the freezer. Stock cubes vary in quality but I do keep some on hand for emergencies.

Winter Vegetable Broth

Serves 4

This hearty soup draws its inspiration from the Scottish classic, cock-a-leekie, but of course comes without the chicken!

1 tablespoon olive oil	*50 g (2 oz) pearl barley*
2 leeks, sliced	*1.2 litres (2 pints) vegetable stock*
1 large carrot, cubed	*(see page 186)*
1 medium turnip, cubed	*8 no-need-to-soak prunes*
2 medium potatoes, cubed	*salt and freshly ground black pepper*
100 g (4 oz) spring greens, shredded	*chopped fresh parsley to serve*

1. Heat the oil in a large pan, add all the vegetables and cook over a medium heat for 5 minutes without browning. Add the barley and continue cooking for 1 minute.

2. Stir in the stock and seasoning and bring to the boil. Cover and simmer for 45 minutes until the barley and vegetables are tender. About 5 minutes before the end of cooking, stir in the prunes. Adjust the seasoning and serve sprinkled with parsley.

Non-vegetarian Tip

ADD 225 G (8 OZ) DICED STREAKY BACON WITH THE VEGETABLES AND COOK AS ABOVE.

GREEN SUMMER SOUP WITH MINT PESTO

Serves 4

I have been making a version of this recipe since I first started cooking with Katie Stewart's Times Cookery Book *as my guide. She had a wonderful recipe for cucumber vichyssoise which I have gradually changed over the years until it metamorphosed into this soup. I usually make it with peas, watercress and leeks but add any other summer vegetables I have left in the vegetable basket. Courgettes and broad beans work well.*

225 g (8 oz) fresh or frozen peas	salt and freshly ground black pepper
1 bunch watercress	dash of dry sherry to serve
2 medium leeks, sliced	
1 medium potato, cubed	FOR THE MINT PESTO
50 g (2oz) butter	6 tablespoons roughly chopped fresh mint
900 ml (1½ pints) vegetable stock	15 g (½ oz) blanched almonds,
(see page 186)	chopped
300 ml (½ pint) semi-skimmed milk	2 tablespoons olive oil

1. Place the peas, watercress, leeks, potato and butter in a large pan, cover and cook gently for 10 minutes until the vegetables are almost tender. Remove the pan from the heat and stir in the stock, milk and seasoning. Bring to the boil, stirring, then cover and simmer for a further 15 minutes until the vegetables are cooked.

2. Meanwhile, make the pesto. Place the mint and almonds in a blender or food processor and process until finely chopped. Add the olive oil and some seasoning and process again until combined.

3. Cool the soup slightly, then purée in a blender or food processor until smooth. Check the seasoning and leave to cool. Chill until ready to serve.

4. To serve, stir the sherry into the soup, pour into bowls and add a swirl of mint pesto. Olive bread makes a good accompaniment.

CURRIED PUMPKIN SOUP

I find that this simple, warming soup is just the thing to serve for Hallowe'en, as it uses up the insides of those endless pumpkin lanterns my children insist on making.

450 g (1lb) pumpkin flesh, cubed	*1 teaspoon mild curry paste*
225 g (8 oz) celeriac, cubed	*25 g (1oz) butter, diced*
1.5 litres (2½ pints) vegetable stock	*salt and freshly ground black pepper*
(see page 186)	

1. Place the pumpkin, celeriac and stock in a large saucepan, stir in the curry paste and seasoning and bring to the boil. Simmer for 20 minutes or until the vegetables are tender.

2. Process the soup in a blender or food processor until smooth, then return it to the pan and reheat until almost boiling. Gradually whisk in the butter until completely incorporated. Serve immediately.

CURRIED PUMPKIN SOUP WITH WALNUT AND CHIVE LOAF (SEE PAGE 179).

DOUBLE-GINGERED TOMATO BROTH

Serves 4

Fresh and ground ginger both add their distinctive flavours to this soup.
If you can't find ripe, well-flavoured fresh tomatoes,
use a can of Italian tomatoes instead.

25 g (1 oz) butter	1 teaspoon ground ginger
1 small onion, chopped	1 tablespoon tomato purée
2 celery sticks, chopped	600 ml (1 pint) vegetable stock
1 medium carrot, chopped	(see page 186)
1 teaspoon grated fresh root ginger	300 ml (½ pint) orange juice
25 g (1 oz) plain flour	salt and freshly ground black pepper
450 g (1 lb) ripe tomatoes,	thick yoghurt and finely shredded
chopped	orange rind to serve

1. Heat the butter in a medium pan, add the onion, celery, carrot and fresh ginger and cook gently for 5 minutes until softened. Add the flour and cook, stirring, until lightly browned.

2. Stir in the tomatoes, ground ginger and tomato purée, followed by the vegetable stock and orange juice. Bring to the boil, then reduce the heat and simmer for 30 minutes.

3. Process the soup in a blender or food processor, then pass through a fine sieve. Return to the clean pan and season to taste. Reheat gently and serve garnished with a spoonful of yoghurt and a scattering of orange rind.

FENNEL SOUP WITH PARMESAN BISCUITS

....

Serves 4

The delicate aniseed flavour of fennel works well in a soup but if it's not to your taste celery can be used instead. To save time, make up a batch of the biscuits ahead and freeze them – they also make a wonderful snack with pre-dinner drinks.

25 g (1 oz) butter	FOR THE BISCUITS
1 small onion, sliced	50 g (2 oz) butter
2 medium fennel bulbs, cut into chunks	50 g (2 oz) self-raising flour
50 g (2 oz) blanched almonds	25 g (1 oz) semolina
600 ml (1 pint) vegetable stock (see page 186)	50 g (2 oz) Parmesan, freshly grated
300 ml (½ pint) single cream	pinch of mustard powder
fennel fronds and toasted almonds	salt and freshly ground black pepper
to garnish	blanched almonds for topping

1. First prepare the biscuits. Preheat the oven to 180°C (350°F, Gas Mark 4). Beat the butter until soft, then work in the flour, semolina, cheese, mustard powder and seasoning to give a soft dough. Wrap and chill for 30 minutes.

2. Roll the dough into walnut-sized balls and press an almond into the top of each one. Place well apart on a greased baking sheet and bake for 15 minutes until pale golden. Cool on a wire rack.

3. For the soup, melt the butter in a large pan, add the onion and fennel and cook for 3 minutes. Stir in the almonds and stock, bring to the boil and simmer for 30 minutes until the fennel is tender. Process in a blender or food processor until smooth and return to a clean pan. Stir in the cream and seasoning and reheat gently – do not allow to boil.

4. To serve, ladle the soup into serving bowls and sprinkle with a few chopped fennel fronds and toasted almonds. Serve with the biscuits.

STILTON AND APPLE SOUP WITH WALNUT CREAM

Serves 6

This soup makes an excellent starter for the Christmas meal.
It's fairly rich so serve small bowlfuls.

25 g (1 oz) butter	*175 g (6 oz) Stilton cheese, crumbled*
1 tablespoon olive oil	*4 tablespoons single cream*
1 small onion, finely chopped	*salt and freshly ground black pepper*
2 celery sticks, chopped	
1 garlic clove, chopped	*FOR THE WALNUT CREAM*
1 eating apple, peeled, cored and chopped	*4 tablespoons crème fraîche*
2 tablespoons plain flour	*25 g (1 oz) walnuts, finely chopped*
150 ml (¼ pint) dry vermouth	*2 tablespoons chopped fresh chives*
900 ml (1½ pints) vegetable stock	
(see page 186)	

1. Heat the butter and oil in a large pan, add the onion, celery, garlic and apple and cook for 5 minutes until softened and golden. Stir in the flour and cook for 1 minute.

2. Gradually stir in the vermouth and stock and bring to the boil, stirring frequently. Season and simmer for 15 minutes until the vegetables are tender.

3. In a food processor or blender, purée the soup with the Stilton until smooth, then return to the clean pan and stir in the cream. Heat through gently but do not allow to boil. Check the seasoning.

4. To serve, mix together the crème fraîche, walnuts and chives. Ladle the soup into serving bowls and float a spoonful of the walnut cream on top.

Beetroot Soup with Horseradish Dumplings

Serves 6

Fresh raw beetroot is now available in supermarkets during the summer and it is far more versatile than you might expect if you have only come across it heavily vinegared in a salad. I bake it whole, make it into chips or use it in this delicately flavoured soup. You really do need to use well-flavoured stock in this recipe. If you can't find fresh horseradish, root ginger also works well in the dumplings.

2 tablespoons olive oil	FOR THE HORSERADISH DUMPLINGS
1 red onion, sliced	50 g (2 oz) plain flour
1 garlic clove, crushed	pinch of salt
350 g (12 oz) fresh beetroot, cut into matchsticks	1 teaspoon grated fresh horseradish
1 teaspoon coarse-grained mustard	25 g (1 oz) vegetable suet
1.2 litres (2 pints) vegetable stock (see page 186)	1 tablespoon chopped fresh flat-leaf parsley
2 tablespoons dry sherry	
salt and freshly ground black pepper	

1. Heat the oil in a pan, add the onion, garlic and beetroot and cook gently for 5 minutes until softened. Add the mustard, stock and seasoning and bring to the boil. Cover and simmer gently for 30 minutes until the beetroot is tender.

2. To make the dumplings, place all the ingredients in a bowl and mix to a soft dough with 2–3 tablespoons cold water. Roll into small balls the size of hazelnuts and drop them into the soup. Simmer gently for 10 minutes until the dumplings are puffed up and cooked. Stir in the sherry, check the seasoning and serve immediately.

Spring Greens Soup with White Beans and Garlic Croutons

Serves 4

This wonderful country-style soup is a meal in itself. Serve with good bread,
follow it with a salad and a fine selection of cheeses, and you and your guests will be
more than satisfied.

2 tablespoons olive oil	*salt and freshly ground black pepper*
1 small onion, finely chopped	*extra virgin olive oil and freshly grated*
1 medium turnip, diced	*Parmesan to serve*
1 medium carrot, diced	
350 g (12 oz) spring greens, shredded	FOR THE CROUTONS
8–10 saffron strands	*2 thick slices country-style bread*
1.2 litres (2 pints) vegetable stock	*2 tablespoons olive oil*
(see page 186)	*1 garlic clove, crushed*
425 g (15 oz) can cannellini beans, drained	

1. Heat the oil in a large pan, add the onion and cook for 3 minutes over a medium heat until softened. Add the turnip, carrot and spring greens and continue cooking until the greens are wilted.

2. Mix the saffron with 3 tablespoons of hot stock and add to the pan with the remaining stock and some seasoning. Bring to the boil and simmer over a low-medium heat for about 20–25 minutes until the vegetables are tender. Stir in the beans and simmer for a further 5 minutes. Check the seasoning.

3. While the soup is cooking, make the croutons. Cut the bread into 2.5 cm (1 in) cubes. Heat the oil in a small frying pan and add the bread and garlic. Fry over a medium heat until golden, remove with a slotted spoon and drain on kitchen paper.

4. Scatter the croutons over the soup and serve drizzled with extra virgin olive oil and sprinkled with freshly grated Parmesan.

Starters and Snacks

ONE COMMON problem when planning vegetarian meals is deciding which dish to serve as the focus and then balancing the rest of the menu. Many of the dishes in a book like this work as a main course or can be adapted to serve as a starter, so how does one decide what to put in a chapter labelled starters? In the end I grouped together recipes that will make life easier for anyone unused to planning a meal without meat or will suit those who simply want to find a snack for a light lunch. In this chapter you'll find a selection of personal favourites that I like to start a meal with – like many cooks, both experienced and otherwise, I often end up serving the same old dishes again and again just because it saves on the planning. And because I like them!

Herbed Drop Scones

Serves 4

You can vary the herbs used for these little pancakes according to your choice of topping. I've used dill with goat's cheese but basil and mozzarella is an obvious alternative. Oregano with tomato and feta, fennel seed pancakes with walnut and stilton, or thyme with a mushroom mixture would all work well.

225 g (8 oz) self-raising flour	freshly ground black pepper
½ teaspoon cream of tartar	sunflower oil for frying
¼ teaspoon bicarbonate of soda	
¼ teaspoon salt	FOR THE TOPPING
pinch of cayenne pepper	1 tablespoon black olive paste
1 egg	100 g (4 oz) goat's cheese, cubed
300 ml (½ pint) semi-skimmed milk	fresh dill sprigs and mixed salad leaves
2–3 tablespoons chopped fresh dill	to garnish

1. Sift the flour, cream of tartar, bicarbonate of soda, salt and cayenne pepper into a mixing bowl. Beat the egg and milk together, make a well in the centre of the dry ingredients and gradually beat in the liquid until you have a smooth batter. Stir in the dill and pepper. Cover the batter and leave to stand for 30 minutes.

2. Heat a little oil in a large frying pan and cook tablespoonfuls of the mixture for about 2 minutes until golden underneath. Turn and cook the other side for 2 minutes. Keep the pancakes warm by wrapping them in a tea towel while you cook the rest.

3. Mix the olive paste and goat's cheese together and pile on to the pancakes. Garnish with fresh dill sprigs and serve on a bed of mixed salad leaves.

HERBED DROP SCONES TOPPED WITH GOAT'S CHEESE, BLACK OLIVE PASTE, TOMATO AND CHILLI SALSA (SEE PAGE 184) AND DILL, AND SERVED WITH ROASTED AUBERGINE MAYONNAISE (SEE PAGE 186).

Spring Onion Cakes

These savoury little cakes make an ideal starter served with a chilli and soy dipping sauce, or they can be handed round with drinks. They are at their best made in advance and fried just before serving but will also keep well, covered, in a warm oven.

225 g (8 oz) plain flour	*4 spring onions, finely chopped*
salt	*sunflower oil for brushing and frying*
1 tablespoon sesame oil	

1. Sieve the flour and a pinch of salt into a mixing bowl. Add the sesame oil and about 250–300 ml (8–10 fl oz) hot water to make a soft dough. Turn on to a lightly floured work surface and knead until no longer sticky, adding a little more oil if the dough gets dry and stiff. Place in a clean bowl and cover with a damp cloth. Leave to stand for 30 minutes.

2. Cut the dough into 8 pieces and roll each one out to a strip about 30 x 4 cm (12 x 1½ in). Brush with a little sunflower oil, then sprinkle with chopped spring onions and salt. Roll up each piece, stand it on one end and press down firmly to make a flat cake.

3. Heat a little oil in a frying pan and cook the cakes for 3 minutes on each side until golden brown. Drain on kitchen paper and serve hot.

MUSHROOM AND GARLIC CROSTINI

Serves 2–4

Crostini is Italian for little toasts; larger versions are known as bruschetta (see page 33). The former make an excellent quick snack or starter, whilst bruschetta are more filling.

½ *large baguette*	*oyster and field mushrooms, sliced*
50 g (2 oz) soft cheese with herbs and garlic	*1 garlic clove, chopped*
	3 tablespoons dry white wine
FOR THE TOPPING	*2 tablespoons chopped fresh parsley*
2 tablespoons olive oil	½ *teaspoon chopped fresh thyme*
225 g (8 oz) mixed mushrooms such as chestnut,	*salt and freshly ground black pepper*

1. First prepare the topping. Heat the oil in a large frying pan, add the mushrooms and garlic and cook for 8–10 minutes, stirring occasionally, until softened. Add the wine and seasoning and simmer to reduce the liquid. Stir in the parsley and thyme.

2. Cut the bread into slices 2–2.5 cm (¾–1 in) thick and toast them. Spread one side with the cheese and top with the mushroom mixture. Serve immediately.

ROASTED BEETROOT WITH SOURED CREAM AND HORSERADISH

Serves 4

Beetroot always reminds me of the salads my grandmother used to make – lettuce, cucumber, tomato and hard-boiled egg with slices of beetroot turning everything purple and adding the overwhelming flavour of vinegar. Luckily it's easy these days to find fresh raw beetroot and start from scratch, and it's wonderful served hot.

4 fresh beetroot	*FOR THE SAUCE*
2 tablespoons olive oil	6 tablespoons crème fraîche
1 teaspoon caraway seeds	1–2 teaspoons horseradish sauce
	2 tablespoons chopped mixed fresh herbs, such as
	chives, dill, parsley and tarragon
	salt and freshly ground black pepper

1. Preheat the oven to 220°C (425°F, Gas Mark 7). Wrap each beetroot in foil and place in a roasting tin. Cook for about 1½ hours until tender.

2. While the beetroot is cooking, make the sauce. Mix together the crème fraîche, horseradish, herbs and seasoning.

3. Remove the beetroot from the oven, open the foil and cut each beetroot into quarters. Arrange on individual serving plates, then drizzle over the olive oil and sprinkle with the caraway seeds. Serve with the sauce.

Double-cooked Goat's Cheese and Watercress Soufflés

Serves 4

Double cooking is a technique to use if you don't want to worry about preparing such a sensitive dish as a soufflé, or if your guests ring at the last minute to let you know they're going to be delayed. The soufflé mixture is cooked as usual but left to sink and cool. It is then turned out and baked again with a creamy sauce. This particular version has proved very popular with my family and friends but you can add any flavourings to the basic mixture. Here it is served with a cheesy sauce; I have also had success with Fresh Tomato Sauce (see page 188).

50 g (2 oz) butter, plus extra for brushing	*4 size-2 eggs, separated*
50 g (2 oz) plain flour	*salt and freshly ground black pepper*
300 ml (½ pint) semi-skimmed milk	
100 g (4 oz) goat's cheese (choose a good tangy one)	*To finish*
1 small bunch watercress, stalks discarded and	*4 tablespoons double cream*
leaves finely chopped	*3 tablespoons freshly grated Parmesan*

1. Preheat the oven to 200°C (400°F, Gas Mark 6). Melt the butter in a small pan until foaming and use a little to brush the insides of four large teacups (don't use your best china!) or 10 cm (4 in) ramekins. Stir the flour into the remaining melted butter. Cook for a minute, then remove the pan from the heat and gradually whisk in the milk. Return the pan to the heat and stir until the sauce is very thick and smooth.

2. Remove the pan from the heat again and crumble in the goat's cheese, followed by the watercress, egg yolks and plenty of seasoning. Whisk the egg whites until stiff but not dry and fold them quickly and lightly into the cheese base. Divide the mixture between the prepared cups or dishes and place on a baking sheet. Cook for 12–14 minutes until well-risen and golden. Remove from the oven and set aside to cool.

3. About 14 minutes before serving, carefully loosen the edges of the soufflés with a knife and turn them out into a buttered shallow ovenproof dish. Spoon a tablespoon of cream over each soufflé and sprinkle with Parmesan. Return to the oven for 8–10 minutes until puffed up and heated through. Serve immediately.

Aubergine Ramekins

Serves 4

Southern Italy is a haven for vegetarians on the lookout for delicious food that doesn't rely on meat for its impact. Flavoursome dishes are prepared from simple ingredients of the highest quality to produce food that is not only appetizing but also wonderful to look at. One of the most famous Sicilian dishes is caponata, an aubergine stew. Here I've devised a version that is enclosed by yet more aubergine and served in individual dishes as a starter. However, the filling is just as good on its own, served with plenty of crusty bread and a salad for supper.

2 large aubergines	*1 tablespoon chopped pine nuts*
6 tablespoons olive oil	*1 tablespoon raisins*
1 small onion, sliced	*1 tablespoon red wine vinegar*
1 celery stick, chopped	*1 teaspoon granulated sugar*
200 g (7 oz) can chopped tomatoes	*salt and freshly ground black pepper*
1 teaspoon chopped capers	*extra virgin olive oil and salad leaves to serve*

1. Cut one of the aubergines lengthways into thin slices. Heat 2 tablespoons of the oil in a frying pan and fry the aubergine slices on both sides until crisp and golden. Drain on kitchen paper, cover and set aside. Cut the other aubergine into small cubes and fry in 2 tablespoons of the remaining oil until lightly browned. Drain on kitchen paper.

2. Heat the remaining oil in a frying pan, add the onion and celery and cook over a medium heat for 5 minutes until softened and just beginning to brown. Add the tomatoes and simmer for about 10 minutes until they form a thick sauce. Stir in the capers, pine nuts, raisins, vinegar, sugar and seasoning and cook for a further 5 minutes. Stir in the cubed aubergine.

3. Line four 8 cm (3 in) oiled ramekins with the aubergine slices, pressing them together so there are no gaps and letting the slices hang over the edge. Spoon the filling into the lined ramekins and fold over the aubergine to enclose the filling. Cover tightly with non-pvc cling wrap and chill for several hours.

4. To serve, turn the ramekins out on to individual serving plates, pour over a little extra virgin olive oil and garnish with salad leaves.

BETTY'S PESTO AND MOZZARELLA ROLLS

Serves 1

This recipe is a tribute to Betty's of York, the famous tearooms where I ate the original of this recipe. If you are in York or near one of their other shops in Yorkshire, go in and buy their olive rolls to use for this.

1 black olive roll or ciabatta roll	50 g (2 oz) mozzarella, sliced
1 teaspoon pesto sauce (see page 188)	1 teaspoon extra virgin olive oil
1 ripe tomato, sliced	salt and freshly ground black pepper

1. Preheat the oven to 200°C (400°F, Gas Mark 6). Split the roll in half and toast it on both sides. Spread the bottom half with the pesto sauce and arrange the sliced tomato and cheese on top. Season to taste.

2. Drizzle the oil over the cut side of the other half of the roll and place it on top of the cheese. Put it in the oven for 5 minutes until the cheese just starts to melt. Serve immediately.

Roasted Peppers with Mozzarella

Serves 4

While writing this book I've had to keep a firm check on the number of recipes containing peppers and aubergines, since they are two of my favourite vegetables and I also have a family of fanatic pepper and aubergine fans at home, clamouring for new ideas.
I know there are people who can't abide either so I apologize to them for the regularity with which they appear in my recipes. If you are not sure about peppers, do try this dish; roasting not only brings out their sweetness it also makes it easy to remove the skins, which many find indigestible. It makes a colourful starter or summer lunch or supper dish. Use really good olive oil and serve it with plenty of bread so that you don't miss out on the wonderful juices.

4 large peppers, red, yellow or orange	175 g (6 oz) mozzarella (buffalo mozzarella if
2 sun-dried tomatoes in olive oil, shredded	you can get it), sliced
2 garlic cloves, thinly sliced	6–8 fresh basil leaves, torn into pieces
4 tablespoons extra virgin olive oil	salt and freshly ground black pepper
1 tablespoon balsamic vinegar	

1. Preheat the oven to 220°C (425°F, Gas Mark 7). Place the peppers on a baking sheet and cook for 20–25 minutes until the skins are blackened. Place in a plastic bag for 5 minutes for the skins to loosen.

2. Skin, halve and deseed the peppers and cut them into strips. Place in a bowl with the sun-dried tomatoes and garlic. Whisk together the olive oil, vinegar and seasoning and pour over the peppers. Leave to cool to room temperature.

3. Just before serving, stir the mozzarella and basil into the pepper mixture and check the seasoning, then pile them on to a serving dish and serve.

Non-vegetarian Tip

ADD 6 CHOPPED ANCHOVY FILLETS TO THE PEPPERS WITH THE SUN-DRIED TOMATOES AND GARLIC.

ROASTED PEPPERS WITH MOZZARELLA SERVED WITH ROSEMARY FOCACCIA ROLLS (SEE PAGE 181).

Herbed Soft Cheese with Green Peppercorns

Serves 4–6

This fresh-tasting home-made cheese is very simple to prepare because it is based on yoghurt. By making your own soft cheese you can add flavourings such as fresh herbs, which make all the difference. The cheese can be served as a starter or as part of a cheeseboard.

450 g (1 lb) Greek yoghurt	1 tablespoon chopped fresh tarragon
1 garlic clove, crushed	1 tablespoon chopped fresh flat-leaf parsley
1 teaspoon green peppercorns (in brine, not dried), crushed	salt and freshly ground black pepper
	vegetable crudités, such as cucumber, celery,
2 tablespoons chopped fresh chives	carrot, peppers, etc., to serve

1. Place the yoghurt in a bowl and stir in the garlic, peppercorns, herbs and seasoning. Mix well and spoon into the centre of a double thickness of muslin or a clean J-cloth. Draw the edges together to form a bag and tie securely with string.

2. Hang the bag in a cool place with a bowl placed underneath to catch any drips (I find the easiest way to do this is to suspend it from a cupboard door handle) and leave for 24 hours until the cheese is firm. Chill until ready to serve.

3. To serve, open the cloth and carefully peel it away from the cheese. Place on a serving dish and serve with a selection of vegetable crudités.

Scrambled Eggs with Feta and Green Beans

Serves 4

Runner beans are one of the joys of summer, especially when freshly picked from the garden. This colourful starter is quick to prepare and it also makes an excellent light supper.

350 g (12 oz) runner beans	25 g (1 oz) butter
6 eggs	2 tablespoons single cream
1 tablespoon chopped fresh tarragon	100 g (4 oz) feta cheese, cubed
2 tablespoons chopped fresh chives	salt and freshly ground black pepper
2 sun-dried tomatoes in olive oil, shredded	

1. Shred the runner beans or cut them into thin lengths using a bean slicer. Cook in boiling water for 5 minutes until just tender. Drain, arrange in a warmed serving dish and keep warm.

2. Beat the eggs with the herbs, sun-dried tomatoes and seasoning. Heat the butter in a non-stick pan until foaming, then add the egg mixture and cream and stir over a gentle heat until just set. Stir in the feta cheese.

3. Spoon the egg mixture over the beans and serve immediately.

BRUSCHETTA WITH PARSLEY AND RED ONION

Serves 4

In its simplest form, bruschetta is just toasted bread rubbed with a little garlic and drizzled with olive oil. As such, it's well worth using the finest ingredients in order to appreciate it at its best. Extra flavourings can be added, such as those suggested here. You could serve the bruschetta cut into small pieces with drinks or as a starter or snack.

1 medium red onion, chopped	*1 garlic clove, chopped*
2 sun-dried tomatoes in olive oil, finely chopped	*4 tablespoons extra virgin olive oil*
1 tablespoon capers, finely chopped	*4 thick slices open-textured bread*
5 tablespoons chopped fresh flat-leaf parsley	*salt and freshly ground black pepper*

1. Put all the ingredients except the bread in a bowl and mix well.

2. Toast the bread on both sides. While it is still hot, divide the topping between the slices and serve.

Vegetable Fritters with Lemon Aioli

Serves 4

Use any seasonal vegetables for this dish – I like a mixture of fennel, courgette and red pepper for colour and flavour.

680 g (1½ lb) mixed seasonal vegetables, such as fennel, courgette, cauliflower, carrot, sweet potato, onion, etc.	FOR THE AIOLI
	2–3 garlic cloves, peeled
	large pinch of cayenne pepper
25 g (1 oz) plain flour	1 egg yolk
1 egg white	grated rind and juice of ½ lemon
sunflower oil for deep frying	150 ml (¼ pint) olive oil
chives	salt and freshly ground black pepper

1. First prepare the aioli. Place the garlic cloves in a pestle and mortar with the cayenne and a large pinch of salt and crush to a paste. Mix with the egg yolk in a small bowl and stir in the lemon rind and juice. Gradually add the oil, drop by drop, whisking continuously, until you have a thick, glossy sauce. Check the seasoning and transfer to a serving dish.

2. Cut the vegetables into slices about 5–10 mm (¼–½ inch) thick, cutting carrots and courgettes on the diagonal. Cut cauliflower into small florets. Just before serving, heat the oil until it is hot enough to brown a small cube of bread in 30 seconds. Season the flour and then toss the vegetables lightly in it to coat. Whisk the egg white until fairly stiff and quickly dip the vegetable slices in it.

3. Fry the vegetables in batches in the hot oil for 3–4 minutes until golden. Drain well on kitchen paper and serve immediately, scattered with chives, with the aioli.

VEGETABLE FRITTERS WITH LEMON AIOLI.

ROSEMARY PIZZELLE WITH TOMATO SAUCE AND ROCKET

Serves 4

These baby pizzas are fried and served piping hot with a topping spooned over them. I discovered them in Sicily, where they are served with wonderfully rich sauces and seem to epitomize the flavours of the island.

	For the sauce
225 g (8 oz) strong plain flour	
½ sachet easy-blend yeast	3 tablespoons olive oil
1 teaspoon salt	1 garlic clove, finely chopped
2 tablespoons chopped fresh rosemary	400 g (14 oz) can chopped tomatoes
1 tablespoon olive oil	1 teaspoon dried oregano
sunflower oil for deep frying	salt and freshly ground black pepper
200 g (7 oz) bag rocket leaves to serve	

1. Sift the flour into a bowl and stir in the yeast, salt and rosemary. Mix the olive oil with 150 ml (¼ pint) hand-hot water, stir it into the flour and mix to a soft dough. Turn on to a floured surface and knead for 5–10 minutes until the dough is soft and elastic. Place in an oiled bowl, cover and leave in a warm place for about 45 minutes or until doubled in size.

2. To make the sauce, heat the olive oil in a small pan, add the garlic and cook for 1 minute until golden. Add the tomatoes, oregano and seasoning and simmer for 15–20 minutes until the sauce has thickened.

3. Turn the dough on to a lightly floured surface and knead lightly. With floured hands, tear off small pieces of dough about the size of a golf ball and shape them into little flat discs about 8 cm (3 in) in diameter. You should have about 12–16. Arrange on a floured tea towel.

4. To cook the pizzelle, heat a large pan of oil until almost smoking and deep fry them a few at a time until golden – they should only take a couple of minutes. Drain on kitchen paper.

5. To serve, arrange a bed of rocket leaves on each plate, place the pizzelle on top and pour over the sauce. Serve immediately.

SPICED MUSHROOMS

Serves 4

This dish is marvellous hot or cold with plenty of crusty bread to soak up the juices.
It is well worth using shallots for the wonderful flavour they give but if you can't get them
button onions will do instead. Shallots can be very difficult to peel. However, if you place
them in a bowl, cover with boiling water for a minute or two, then drain,
the skins should come off easily.

225 g (8 oz) shallots, peeled	*4 tablespoons red wine vinegar*
6 tablespoons olive oil	*1 garlic clove, crushed*
1 teaspoon caster sugar	*1 teaspoon tomato purée*
350 g (12 oz) small chestnut mushrooms	*sprig of fresh thyme*
¼ teaspoon coriander seeds	*salt and freshly ground black pepper*
large pinch of cayenne pepper	*chopped fresh parsley to garnish*
1 bay leaf	

1. Place the shallots in a pan of water, bring to the boil and simmer for 5 minutes. Drain and pat dry. Heat 2 tablespoons of the oil in a frying pan, add the shallots and sugar and cook gently for 7–8 minutes until just golden. Add the mushrooms and coriander seeds and cook over a high heat for a couple of minutes. Don't overcook the mushrooms or they will be flabby.

2. While the vegetables are cooking, place the remaining olive oil in a mixing bowl with the cayenne, bay leaf, vinegar, garlic, tomato purée, thyme and seasoning. Whisk to combine, then add the warm shallots and mushrooms and mix well. Leave to cool, stirring occasionally. Serve garnished with chopped parsley.

Goat's Cheese Filo Parcels

Serves 4

You can substitute good-quality olive paste for the pesto in these little pastry parcels.
Make larger versions for a main course.

175 g (6 oz) firm goat's cheese, rind removed	1 tablespoon pesto sauce
50 g (2 oz) full-fat soft cheese	(see page 188)
2 tablespoons chopped fresh chives	225 g (8 oz) bag mixed salad leaves
1 tablespoon chopped fresh tarragon	3 tablespoons Olive Oil Dressing
4 sheets filo pastry, about 20 x 30 cm	(see page 189)
(8 x 12 in)	15 g (½ oz) pine nuts, toasted
25 g (1 oz) butter, melted	salt and freshly ground black pepper

1. Preheat the oven to 200°C (400°F, Gas Mark 6). Place the goat's cheese in a bowl with the soft cheese, herbs and seasoning and cream together until combined. Divide into four and shape into cubes.

2. Brush each sheet of filo with melted butter and fold in half to form a 20 x 15 cm (8 x 6 in) rectangle. Brush with butter again. Place some pesto in the centre of each piece of filo and top with a cube of the cheese mixture. Fold up the pastry to form a neat parcel and place on a baking sheet. Brush with melted butter.

3. Cook the cheese parcels for 15–20 minutes until golden and crisp. Toss the salad leaves with the dressing and pine nuts and divide between four individual serving plates. Top each one with a filo parcel and serve immediately.

Pasta and Rice

PASTA AND RICE have become the mainstay of many a meal in the UK, vegetarian or otherwise – not surprising when you consider the enormous versatility of both of these staples and their key role in cuisines around the world. High in complex carbohydrates, low in fat, and inexpensive, they fit with ease into the modern way of cooking and eating. Both can be happily paired with almost any ingredient to produce an infinite variety of dishes, from the everyday to the sophisticated.

The correct cooking method is vital to the success of any dish made with pasta or rice. The former becomes sticky and flabby when overcooked, the latter mushy – neither is to be recommended. Pasta should be tender but not soft, while rice should be fluffy with each grain separate, unless you are cooking risotto rice which should be creamy. One tip, and this is especially useful if you have problems when cooking rice, is always to use the biggest pan available and plenty of cooking water (salt the water for pasta). Bring the water to the boil, then pour in the rice or pasta and stir once. Return the water to a gentle rolling boil and cook at that pace until just tender. Always taste to check if your pasta or rice is ready – don't rely on the cooking time on the packet as it's just a guide. Pour a little cold water directly into the pan to stop any further cooking and then drain. Pour a kettle of boiling water over rice and leave to drain for five minutes.

Mushroom and Leek Macaroni

Serves 4

Macaroni cheese gets the vote as my favourite TV dinner and brings back memories of communal living when I started work in London and was sharing my first flat. A bowl of macaroni in a really cheesy sauce with frozen peas on the side made the perfect partner for the latest episode of 'Dallas'. My children are now also fans (of macaroni cheese, not 'Dallas'!) and this version, which is cooked on a base of vegetables, is a surefire way of getting them to eat extra vegetables without noticing.

275 g (10 oz) macaroni or penne	FOR THE SAUCE
25 g (1 oz) butter	25 g (1 oz) butter
1 large leek, thinly sliced	25 g (1 oz) plain flour
225 g (8 oz) chestnut mushrooms, sliced	450 ml (¾ pint) semi-skimmed milk
1 red pepper, seeded and sliced	100 g (4 oz) mature Cheddar, grated
25 g (1 oz) fresh brown breadcrumbs	1 teaspoon English mustard
2 tablespoons freshly grated Parmesan	3 tablespoons crème fraîche
pinch of cayenne pepper	salt and freshly ground black pepper
2 tablespoons chopped fresh parsley	

1. Preheat the oven to 200°C (400°F, Gas Mark 6). Bring a large pan of salted water to the boil, add the pasta and cook for 8–10 minutes until just tender. Drain.

2. While the pasta is cooking, melt the butter in a large frying pan, add the leek, mushrooms and red pepper and cook over a medium heat for 5 minutes until softened. Season well and place in a large, shallow ovenproof dish. Arrange the pasta on top of the vegetables.

3. Prepare the sauce. Melt the butter in a medium pan, add the flour and cook for 1 minute. Remove from the heat and gradually whisk in the milk, then return to the heat and bring to the boil, stirring continuously, to give a thick, smooth sauce. Simmer for 2 minutes, then remove from the heat again and stir in the cheese, mustard, crème fraîche and seasoning. Pour the sauce over the pasta.

4. Mix together the breadcrumbs, Parmesan, cayenne and parsley and scatter them over the sauce. Bake for 15–20 minutes until the top is golden. Serve immediately.

Spaghetti Squash and Noodles Milanese

Serves 4

My children are fascinated by the way the flesh of the spaghetti squash breaks into strands when it's cooked, and as a result will eat it quite happily without a murmur. Combined with green and white tagliarini and flavoured with saffron and Parmesan, it makes a delicate yet satisfying starter or light supper.

1 spaghetti squash, about 680 g (1½ lb)	¼ teaspoon saffron strands
350 g (12 oz) green and yellow fresh tagliarini	3 tablespoons shredded fresh basil
50 g (2 oz) butter	salt and freshly ground black pepper
1 shallot, finely chopped	freshly grated Parmesan to serve
4 tablespoons dry white wine	

1. Pierce the spaghetti squash several times with a skewer, then cook it in a large pan of simmering water for about 35–40 minutes until tender. Drain the squash, cut it in half lengthways and discard the seeds. Using a fork, pull out the strands of flesh and place them in a warm serving dish.

2. Cook the pasta in plenty of boiling salted water for about 3 minutes until just tender. Drain and mix with the squash.

3. Melt the butter in a small pan, add the shallot and cook for a couple of minutes until softened. Add the wine and saffron and simmer until the liquid is reduced by half.

4. Pour the hot butter over the pasta, add the basil and seasoning and toss gently. Serve with grated Parmesan.

Roasted Aubergine and Olive Lasagne

Serves 6

I like to use fresh lasagne from an Italian delicatessen for this dish but the dried variety that needs no pre-cooking will work too. Just remember to make the sauce thinner by adding extra milk, as the dried pasta will soak up more liquid as it cooks.

2 large aubergines, about 450 g/1lb in total, sliced lengthways	*2 tablespoons freshly grated Parmesan to finish*
4 tablespoons olive oil	
2 tablespoons olive paste	*For the béchamel sauce*
350 g (12 oz) fresh lasagne	*25 g (1 oz) butter*
2 x 400 g (14 oz) cans chopped tomatoes	*25 g (1 oz) plain flour*
175 g (6 oz) mozzarella, grated	*450 ml (¾ pint) semi-skimmed milk*
40 g (1½ oz) Parmesan, freshly grated	*freshly grated nutmeg*
2 tablespoons chopped fresh oregano	*4 fresh bay leaves*
salt and freshly ground black pepper	

1. Preheat the oven to 200°C (400°F, Gas Mark 6). Brush the aubergine slices with the olive oil, place on a baking sheet and bake for 20 minutes until golden brown. Spread a little olive paste over one side of each aubergine slice.

2. Cook the lasagne in a large pan of boiling salted water for 2–3 minutes until *al dente*. Drain, rinse under cold running water and pat dry.

3. Spread some of the chopped tomatoes over the base of a 25 cm (10 in) square ovenproof dish and arrange a layer of lasagne on top, taking care that the pasta reaches the edges of the dish but doesn't overlap. Spread with a little more tomato, then a layer of aubergine slices. Sprinkle with grated mozzarella, Parmesan and a little chopped oregano. Season well. Carry on layering the ingredients in this way, finishing with a layer of pasta.

4. Make the béchamel sauce. Melt the butter in a pan, add the flour and cook for a minute. Remove from the heat and gradually whisk in the milk, then return to the heat and bring to the boil, stirring, until thickened and smooth. Simmer for 3 minutes, then season with nutmeg, salt and pepper. Pour the sauce over the lasagne and arrange the bay leaves on the top. Sprinkle with Parmesan and bake for 25–30 minutes until the top is golden. Serve with a green salad and Italian bread.

Roasted Aubergine and Olive Lasagne.

Pasta with Mushrooms and Broad Beans

Serves 4

Only make this dish when you have the smallest, freshest broad beans, preferably picked by yourself from the garden or a pick-your-own farm that same day.

15 g (½ oz) dried porcini mushrooms	1 garlic clove, crushed
100 g (4 oz) podded broad beans	2 tablespoons chopped fresh basil
(about 450 g (1lb) in the pod)	225 g (8 oz) chestnut mushrooms, thickly sliced
350 g (12 oz) pasta shells	4 tablespoons crème fraîche
2 tablespoons olive oil	25 g (1 oz) Parmesan, freshly grated
15 g (½ oz) butter	salt and freshly ground black pepper

1. Cover the dried porcini with hot water and leave to soak for 15 minutes. Drain, squeeze dry and chop them roughly. Cook the broad beans in boiling water for 3 minutes until just tender, then drain and refresh under cold water.

2. Bring a large pan of salted water to the boil, add the pasta and cook for 8–10 minutes or until *al dente*. Drain.

3. While the pasta is cooking, heat the oil and butter in a large frying pan, add the garlic and basil and cook over a high heat for 1 minute. Add the chestnut mushrooms and the chopped porcini, season and cook over a medium-high heat for 5 minutes until the mushrooms are golden. Stir in the broad beans and heat through.

4. Mix the crème fraîche with the Parmesan, stir it into the mushroom mixture and bring to the boil. Pour the sauce over the drained pasta, toss until the pasta is well-coated and serve immediately.

Non-vegetarian Tip

ADD 175 G (6 OZ) DICED STREAKY BACON TO THE PAN WITH THE MUSHROOMS AND CONTINUE AS ABOVE.

Tagliarini with Caramelized Onion and Pine Nuts

Serves 4

This is an intensely flavoured pasta dish that I would follow with a large mixed salad and cheese for a simple supper to serve after a day's work.

2 tablespoons olive oil	350 g (12 oz) egg tagliarini
25 g (1 oz) butter	4 tablespoons chopped fresh flat-leaf parsley
3 large onions, sliced	25 g (1 oz) pine nuts, toasted
1 tablespoon caster sugar	50 g (2 oz) Gruyère cheese, grated
1 tablespoon balsamic vinegar	salt and freshly ground black pepper

1. Heat the oil and butter in a large frying pan, add the sliced onions and cook slowly over a gentle heat for about 30 minutes, stirring occasionally, until really soft. Add the sugar and vinegar, raise the heat and cook for a further 5 minutes until golden.

2. While the onions are cooking, bring a large pan of salted water to the boil, add the pasta and cook for about 5 minutes until *al dente*. Drain thoroughly.

3. Stir the parsley, pine nuts, cheese and seasoning into the onions and pour this mixture over the pasta. Toss gently to coat the pasta in the sauce and serve.

SPAGHETTI WITH WALNUT HERB BUTTER

Serves 4

Toasting the walnuts first brings out their flavour to the full but if you're in a hurry you can leave out this step. Vegans could substitute 6 tablespoons olive oil for the butter and omit the Parmesan.

350 g (12 oz) spaghetti	parsley, chives, basil, tarragon and chervil
50 g (2 oz) walnut pieces	1 teaspoon grated lemon rind
25 g (1 oz) shelled pistachio nuts	salt and freshly ground black pepper
75 g (3 oz) butter, diced	freshly grated Parmesan to serve
25 g (1 oz) chopped mixed fresh herbs, such as	

1. Bring a large pan of salted water to the boil and cook the spaghetti for 8–10 minutes until *al dente*. Drain and return to the pan.

2. While the pasta is cooking, place the walnuts in a frying pan and dry fry for a couple of minutes until golden. Put them in a blender or food processor with the pistachio nuts, butter, herbs and lemon rind. Add plenty of seasoning and process until well combined, leaving the mixture slightly crunchy if you prefer.

3. Add the walnut butter to the hot pasta and toss to coat completely. Serve with freshly grated Parmesan.

PASTA WITH SPRING VEGETABLES

This fresh-tasting pasta dish makes a lovely starter before a heavy main course or an ideal quick supper for casual visitors. Use a well-flavoured stock and make sure the vegetables are as fresh as possible to give the sauce the right depth of flavour.

100 g (4 oz) asparagus tips	*3 tablespoons extra virgin olive oil*
100 g (4 oz) baby carrots	*1 medium tomato, skinned,*
100 g (4 oz) baby leeks	*seeded and chopped*
100 g (4 oz) small broccoli florets	*2 tablespoons chopped fresh chives*
300 ml (½ pint) vegetable stock	*350 g (12 oz) egg tagliarini*
(see page 186)	*salt and freshly ground black pepper*

1. Blanch all the vegetables in boiling water for a couple of minutes until just tender. Plunge them into cold water, drain and pat dry. Cut the asparagus, carrots and leeks into 5 cm (2 in) lengths on the diagonal.

2. Put the stock in a medium pan and boil until reduced to a third of its original volume; it should have a syrupy consistency. Place in a blender and, with the motor running, drizzle in the olive oil to make an emulsified sauce. Return the sauce to the pan, stir in the tomato and chives and keep warm.

3. Cook the pasta in plenty of boiling salted water until *al dente*, then drain. Add it to the sauce with the vegetables and stir over a low heat to warm through. Season to taste and serve immediately.

PASTA WITH SPRING VEGETABLES.

Aubergine and Tomato Timbale

Serve this spectacular dish when cooking for crowds, as it looks impressive, can be made well in advance and heated through, and is easy to eat with a fork. It originates from Sicily, where aubergines, tomatoes and fresh basil are ubiquitous, especially with pasta.

4 tablespoons olive oil	*50 g (2 oz) stoned black olives, chopped*
2 garlic cloves, chopped	*150 g (5 oz) mozzarella cheese, grated*
4 tablespoons chopped fresh basil	*25 g (1 oz) Parmesan, freshly grated*
1 dried chilli, chopped	*1 teaspoon dried oregano*
400 g (14 oz) can chopped tomatoes	*salt and freshly ground black pepper*
2 large aubergines, sliced into thin rounds	*sunflower oil for frying*
450 g (1 lb) penne	

1. First make a tomato sauce. Heat half the olive oil in a medium pan, add the garlic, basil and chilli and cook for 1 minute until golden. Stir in the tomatoes and seasoning and simmer for 20–25 minutes until the sauce has thickened.

2. Preheat the oven to 200°C (400°F, Gas Mark 6). Heat about 2.5 cm (1 in) sunflower oil in a frying pan and fry the aubergine slices in batches until golden on both sides. Drain thoroughly on kitchen paper.

3. Cook the pasta in plenty of boiling salted water for 8–10 minutes until *al dente*. Drain well and toss in the remaining olive oil. Mix the pasta with the tomato sauce, olives, cheeses, oregano and seasoning.

4. Use the aubergine slices to line the base and sides of a greased, spring-release 20 cm (8 in) cake tin, then spoon the pasta mixture into the centre. Arrange the rest of the aubergine slices on top and press down lightly. Bake for 25 minutes until piping hot. Turn out on to a warmed serving dish and serve cut into wedges.

Goat's Cheese and Pesto Lasagne

Serves 6

This recipe uses a classic basil pesto which gives it a wonderfully fresh flavour.

350 g (12 oz) fresh lasagne verde	FOR THE BÉCHAMEL SAUCE
100 g (4 oz) pesto sauce (see page 188)	50 g (2 oz) butter
100 g (4 oz) ricotta cheese	50 g (2 oz) plain flour
100 g (4 oz) firm goat's cheese, crumbled	600 ml (1 pint) milk
25 g (1 oz) Parmesan, freshly grated	freshly grated nutmeg
50 g (2 oz) pine nuts, toasted	salt and freshly ground black pepper
2 tablespoons freshly grated Parmesan	
to finish	

1. Preheat the oven to 190°C (375°F, Gas Mark 5). Cook the lasagne in a large pan of boiling salted water for 2–3 minutes until *al dente*. Drain, rinse under cold running water and pat dry.

2. Next make the béchamel sauce. Melt the butter in a medium pan, add the flour and cook, stirring, for 1 minute. Remove from the heat and gradually whisk in the milk, then return to the heat and bring to the boil, stirring constantly. Simmer for 3 minutes until the sauce is the consistency of thin cream. Season with salt, pepper and nutmeg.

3. Spread a little of the sauce over the base of a 20 x 30 cm (8 x 12 in) baking dish, then spoon over 1 tablespoon of the pesto. Arrange a layer of pasta sheets on top, trying not to overlap them. Spread a thin layer of pesto over the pasta, then scatter over some of the ricotta, goat's cheese, Parmesan and pine nuts. Pour a thin layer of béchamel over the top.

4. Continue layering the ingredients in this way, finishing with a layer of pasta and a final layer of béchamel. Scatter over the extra Parmesan and cook for 30–35 minutes until the top is golden and bubbling. Serve immediately, with a tomato salad.

Tagliatelle with Tomato and Grilled Artichoke Sauce

Serves 4

If you can find baby artichokes they are well worth buying for this pasta dish because they are tender enough to eat whole, saving on a lot of fiddly preparation. However, canned artichoke hearts work almost as well. Get out your best olive oil for this recipe to complement the flavour of the artichokes.

8 baby artichokes	*1 tablespoon capers, chopped*
3 tablespoons extra virgin olive oil	*4 tablespoons chopped fresh basil*
1 dried red chilli, chopped	*350 g (12 oz) egg tagliatelle*
1 garlic clove, chopped	*salt and freshly ground black pepper*
400 g (14 oz) can tomatoes	

1. Trim the artichoke stalks, remove any tough leaves and cook in boiling water for 10 minutes until almost tender. Drain thoroughly, then brush with a little olive oil and grill under a high heat on all sides until blackened at the edges. Cut into quarters.

2. Heat the remaining olive oil in a medium pan, add the chilli and garlic and cook for a few minutes until golden. Stir in the tomatoes, capers, basil and seasoning and simmer for 25 minutes until the sauce is thick and pulpy. Stir in the artichokes.

3. Cook the tagliatelle in plenty of boiling salted water for 7–8 minutes until *al dente*. Drain and toss with the sauce. Serve immediately.

RICE NOODLES WITH COCONUT AND MANGO

Serves 4

Rice noodles and red curry paste are available from Asian and Thai supermarkets. Check that the version you buy doesn't contain shrimp paste. Red curry paste can be very hot so don't overdo it until you have discovered its level of heat. The noodles are served hot with an uncooked topping which you stir through before eating, giving a pleasing contrast of tastes and textures.

3 tablespoons vegetable oil	350 g (12 oz) rice noodles
1 medium onion, chopped	100 g (4 oz) bean sprouts
2 garlic cloves, chopped	4 spring onions, chopped
1 tablespoon red curry paste, or to taste	1 red pepper, seeded and sliced
300 ml (½ pint) vegetable stock	1 ripe mango, peeled, stoned and cubed
(see page 186)	salt and freshly ground black pepper
300 ml (½ pint) canned coconut milk	

1. Heat the vegetable oil in a deep pan or a wok, add the onion and garlic and stir fry for 5 minutes until golden. Stir in the curry paste and cook for 1 minute. Stir in the stock, coconut milk and seasoning and simmer for 5 minutes.

2. In a separate pan, cook the noodles according to the packet instructions and drain thoroughly. Add them to the coconut liquid and stir to combine. Spoon into individual serving bowls and arrange the bean sprouts, spring onions, pepper and mango on top. Serve immediately.

WHOLEGRAIN RICE PILAFF WITH FENNEL AND ROSEMARY

Serves 4

The strong aniseed flavour of raw fennel is softened by cooking, and in this recipe it is enhanced by the complementary tastes of cider and rosemary. Serve with a salad of bitter leaves.

2 tablespoons olive oil	*300 ml (½ pint) dry cider*
2 fennel bulbs, sliced	*400 g (14 oz) can chopped tomatoes*
1–2 garlic cloves, crushed	*2 tablespoons lemon juice*
350 g (12 oz) wholegrain basmati rice	*salt and freshly ground black pepper*
2 sprigs of fresh rosemary	*fennel fronds to garnish*

1. Preheat the oven to 170°C (325°F, Gas Mark 3). Heat the oil in an ovenproof casserole, add the fennel and garlic and cook for 5 minutes until softened. Add the rice and stir until coated in oil. Stir in the rosemary, cider, tomatoes and seasoning and bring to the boil. Cover the casserole and transfer to the oven.

2. Cook for 1 hour until the rice is tender and all the liquid absorbed. Stir in the lemon juice, check the seasoning and garnish with chopped fennel fronds.

NON-VEGETARIAN TIP

CUT 450 G (1 LB) CHICKEN JOINTS IN HALF AND FRY UNTIL GOLDEN IN 1 TABLESPOON OLIVE OIL. ARRANGE OVER THE TOP OF THE RICE HALFWAY THROUGH COOKING AND THEN STIR IN JUST BEFORE SERVING.

BAKED RICE WITH CHICK PEAS

Serves 4

Rice and pulses is a classic combination in many countries. I found the inspiration for this dish in one of my most-thumbed cookery books, The Foods and Wines of Spain *by Penelope Casas. I make it in a brown earthenware casserole bought specifically for the purpose on a trip to the northwest of Spain last summer, but a heavy flameproof casserole will do just as well.*

3 tablespoons olive oil	*300–450 ml (½–¾ pint) vegetable stock*
1 medium onion, chopped	*(see page 186)*
1 garlic clove, crushed	*salt and freshly ground black pepper*
1 medium tomato, chopped	
225 g (8 oz) potato, cubed	*FOR THE TOPPING*
1 teaspoon paprika	*1 canned pimento, cut into strips*
275 g (10 oz) risotto rice	*6–8 garlic cloves, unpeeled*
3 tablespoons chopped fresh parsley	*2 sun-dried tomatoes in olive oil, sliced*
425 g (15 oz) can chick peas	

1. Heat the oil in a large, shallow flameproof casserole or gratin dish and cook the onion in it over a medium heat for 3 minutes until softened. Add the garlic, tomato and potato and cook for a further 5 minutes, stirring frequently, until just browned. Stir in the paprika, rice and parsley and cook for a couple of minutes until the rice is coated in the oil.

2. Drain the chick peas and make the liquid up to 600 ml (1 pint) with the vegetable stock. Add the chick peas, liquid and seasoning to the pan. Bring to the boil, then arrange the pimento, whole garlic cloves and sun-dried tomatoes on top. Cover the casserole and cook for 20–25 minutes until the rice is tender. Leave to stand, covered, for 5 minutes, then serve with steamed green beans or a crisp salad. The garlic skin can just be pushed away from the cloves as you eat them, and the flesh will be succulent and delicious.

NON-VEGETARIAN TIP

ARRANGE SLICES OF GOOD-QUALITY SPICY CHORIZO SAUSAGE OVER THE TOP OF THE RICE WITH THE PIMENTO AND GARLIC.

ASPARAGUS AND LEMON RISOTTO

Serves 4

The first risotto I ever ate was in Perugia in Italy and it was a revelation. Creamy and delicate, it arrived in a small taster's helping studded with fresh asparagus tips, beside a portion of spinach gnocchi and some pasta. It was quite delicious and I have tried to match it ever since. This recipe includes lemon, which I think works very well. Don't use an over-salty stock as it would spoil the flavour.

350 g (12 oz) asparagus	2 shallots, finely chopped
about 900 ml (1½ pints) vegetable stock	275 g (10 oz) risotto rice
(see page 186)	4 tablespoons freshly grated Parmesan
40 g (1½ oz) butter	salt and freshly ground black pepper
grated rind of 2 lemons	shreds of lemon rind (optional)
2 tablespoons vegetable oil	

1. Bring a large shallow pan of water to the boil, add the asparagus and cook until almost tender. Drain, reserving the cooking liquid, and cut the asparagus into 2.5 cm (1 in) pieces, discarding the tough ends of the stalks. Use the vegetable stock to make up the cooking water to 1.1 litres (2 pints) and heat until simmering.

2. Melt 25 g (1 oz) of the butter in a small pan, add the lemon rind and set aside to infuse. Heat the remaining butter with the oil in a heavy-based pan, add the shallots and cook over a medium heat for 3 minutes until softened. Add the chopped asparagus and heat through, then add the rice and stir until coated in the oil.

3. Stir in the hot stock a ladleful at a time; simmer, stirring constantly, until each addition has been absorbed before adding more stock. Continue in this way until the rice is tender and creamy – this will take about 20 minutes in all. Stir in the lemon butter and Parmesan, season to taste and serve immediately, scattered with shreds of lemon rind.

ASPARAGUS AND LEMON RISOTTO.

TOMATO AND COURGETTE RISOTTO

Serves 4

Risotto is real comfort food but should only be cooked when you are entertaining friends who come and join you in the kitchen as you stir, otherwise you will miss out on all the pre-dinner conversation.

3 tablespoons olive oil	1 litre (1¾ pints) vegetable stock
1 medium onion, finely chopped	(see page 186)
1 garlic clove, crushed	150 ml (¼ pint) dry white wine
3 medium courgettes, chopped	25 g (1 oz) butter
4 sun-dried tomatoes in olive oil,	25 g (1 oz) Parmesan, freshly grated
drained and chopped	2 tablespoons chopped fresh basil
225 g (8 oz) risotto rice	salt and freshly ground black pepper

1. Heat the oil in a heavy-based pan and cook the onion and garlic over a medium heat for 3 minutes until softened. Add the courgettes and continue frying for 5 minutes until lightly browned. Stir in the chopped sun-dried tomatoes. Add the rice and stir to coat with the oil.

2. Heat the stock in a separate pan until simmering. Add 150 ml (¼ pint) of the stock to the rice and simmer over a low-medium heat, stirring constantly, until all the liquid is absorbed. Add 2 more tablespoons of stock and stir until it is absorbed. Continue adding the stock in this way until it is all used up, then add the wine and stir until the rice is creamy-textured and just tender but still has a bite – the total cooking time for the rice should be about 20 minutes.

3. Stir in the butter, Parmesan and basil, season to taste and serve immediately.

ITALIAN RICE AND SPINACH CAKE

Serves 6

*This rice cake makes a wonderful main course for a more formal dinner,
served with Fresh Tomato Sauce (see page 188).*

350 g (12 oz) risotto rice	*150 g (5 oz) buffalo mozzarella, grated*
25 g (1 oz) butter	*50 g (2 oz) pine nuts, toasted and chopped*
50 g (2 oz) Parmesan, freshly grated	*1 shallot, finely chopped*
2 egg yolks	*freshly grated nutmeg*
4 tablespoons double cream	*salt and freshly ground black pepper*
350 g (12 oz) fresh spinach	

1. Preheat the oven to 220°C (425°F, Gas Mark 7). Cook the rice in boiling water for 10 minutes or until just tender. Drain thoroughly and mix with the butter, Parmesan and plenty of seasoning. Beat the egg yolks with the cream and stir into the rice.

2. Wash the spinach and cook in a covered pan with only the water clinging to its leaves for 3–5 minutes until tender. Drain, pressing out any excess liquid, and chop. Mix with the mozzarella, pine nuts and shallot and season with nutmeg, salt and pepper.

3. To assemble, press half the rice mixture into a buttered deep 20 cm (8 in) loose-bottomed cake tin. Spoon the spinach mixture on top and spread level, then top with the rest of the rice. Press down firmly.

4. Cover the tin with foil and bake for 45 minutes until set. Carefully turn out on to a plate and serve cut into wedges.

Thai Rice with Mushrooms and Omelette Strips

Serves 4

Thai jasmine rice should be used in a way that shows off its delicate flavour. Here it is garnished with a chilli and coriander omelette cut into strips, which adds colour and exquisite tastes.

350 g (12 oz) Thai jasmine rice	*For the omelette*
2 tablespoons Kikkoman soy sauce	*2 eggs*
2 tablespoons dry sherry	*2 tablespoons chopped fresh coriander*
1½ tablespoons sunflower oil	*½ red chilli, seeded and finely chopped*
2 spring onions, chopped	*1 tomato, seeded and finely chopped*
1 garlic clove, crushed	*1 teaspoon sunflower oil*
225 g (8 oz) shiitake mushrooms, sliced	*salt and freshly ground black pepper*

1. Rinse the rice under cold running water and place in a heavy-based pan with 600 ml (1 pint) water. Bring to the boil and simmer, uncovered, for about 10 minutes until the surface water has been absorbed. Turn off the heat, cover the pan tightly and set aside.

2. Next make the omelette. Beat the eggs with the coriander, chilli, tomato and seasoning. Heat the oil in an 18 cm (7 in) omelette pan, add the egg mixture and cook until lightly browned on one side. Slide the omelette on to a plate and roll up. Cut into strips.

3. Mix the soy sauce with the sherry and 4 tablespoons water. Heat the oil in a wok or large frying pan and add the spring onions, garlic and mushrooms. Stir fry over a high heat for 3 minutes, then add the soy sauce mixture and simmer for a further 2 minutes.

4. Transfer the rice to a warmed shallow serving dish, spoon over the mushrooms with their juices and arrange the omelette strips on top. Serve immediately.

Non-vegetarian Tip

Marinate 4 skinless boneless chicken breasts in 3 tablespoons soy sauce and 3 tablespoons dry sherry, then grill on both sides until cooked through. Serve with the rice.

Spiced Rice Pilaff with Almonds and Raisins

Serves 4

Soaking basmati rice before cooking gives the finished dish a lighter texture so is well worth doing. I serve this dish as an accompaniment to vegetable curries or as a main dish with a selection of fresh chutneys and Indian breads.

350 g (12 oz) basmati rice	2 carrots, sliced
3 tablespoons vegetable oil	1 small cauliflower, cut into florets
2 medium onions, sliced	900 ml (1½ pints) vegetable stock (see page 186)
1 cm (½ in) piece fresh root ginger, finely chopped	salt
1 green chilli, seeded and chopped	
2 garlic cloves, chopped	To finish
2 teaspoons ground coriander	1 tablespoon vegetable oil
1 teaspoon ground cumin	50 g (2 oz) blanched almonds
½ teaspoon ground turmeric	50 g (2 oz) raisins
1 red pepper, seeded and diced	fresh coriander sprigs to garnish

1. Wash the rice in several changes of water, then cover with fresh water and leave to soak for 30 minutes. Drain.

2. Preheat the oven to 180°C (350°F, Gas Mark 4). Heat half the oil in an ovenproof casserole, add the onions and cook for 5 minutes until golden. Remove half the onion from the pan and continue cooking the rest until really brown and crisp. Remove from the pan and set aside.

3. Heat the remaining oil in the pan, add the softened onion with the ginger, chilli and garlic and cook for 2 minutes, then stir in the spices and cook for 1 minute. Add the vegetables and rice to the pan and stir over a medium heat for a couple of minutes until coated in oil. Season with salt and add the stock. Bring to the boil, cover and transfer to the oven for 25 minutes until the rice and vegetables are tender.

4. To finish the dish, heat the oil in a small pan, add the almonds and stir fry for a couple of minutes until golden. Stir in the raisins and the reserved fried onions, season with salt and fork into the rice. Garnish with fresh coriander and serve.

Non-vegetarian Tip

SERVE WITH TANDOORI CHICKEN OR GRILLED LAMB CHOPS.

RISOTTO CROQUETTES

Serves 4

Leftover risotto, if there is such a thing in your household, makes marvellous little croquettes that can be served as a supper dish or starter. Use any type of risotto, but make sure you store it in the fridge for no longer than 24 hours, as cooked rice can be a source of food poisoning.

225 g (8 oz) leftover risotto	*1 egg, beaten*
50 g (2 oz) smoked mozzarella, cut into 8	*100 g (4 oz) fresh white breadcrumbs*
8 fresh basil leaves	*salt and freshly ground black pepper*
2 tablespoons plain flour	*vegetable oil for frying*

1. Divide the risotto into eight portions and roll them into small croquettes with lightly floured hands. Wrap a cube of mozzarella in a basil leaf and push into the middle of each ball of risotto, then reform the rice around the cheese.

2. Season the flour with salt and pepper. Dip each croquette into the flour, then into the beaten egg and finally into the breadcrumbs.

3. Heat 5 cm (2 in) vegetable oil in a deep frying pan until it is hot enough to brown a small cube of bread in 30 seconds. Add the croquettes and fry for 3–4 minutes, turning to cook both sides. Drain on kitchen paper and serve with Fresh Tomato Sauce (see page 188).

Pastry

Ever since I first started cooking, pastry making has always given me enormous satisfaction. Whether it be a golden-glazed, flaky-topped pie, a creamy-textured flan or a sweet tart, pastry dishes are a pleasure to make and serve. Nowadays I don't have time to start from scratch as often as I'd like so I cut corners with bought pastry and find the results more than satisfactory. I would still always make my own short-crust just because I enjoy the process but there is no reason why you should, and I certainly make full use of filo and puff pastry and always keep them in the freezer.

Pastry dishes are perfect for special-occasion vegetarian meals as they provide a spectacular centrepiece around which to build a menu. Another bonus is that they often freeze well (although some flans become slightly soggy on the base). From a nutritional viewpoint, however, pies and tarts do tend to be high in fat, so make sure the rest of the meal is light and try not to use too many dairy products. If you prefer wholemeal pastry you can substitute wholemeal flour for up to half the amount of white flour given in the recipe but I don't recommend using a greater proportion as I find the results heavy and unmanageable.

Honey-glazed Leek and Parsnip Tart

Serves 4

I think Richard Cawley originally put the idea for this wonderful tart into my head with his description of a savoury version of Tarte Tatin made with parsnips. It's been in the back of my mind ever since, and emerged as this honeyed version. My husband says it's the best dish I've ever cooked for him, which is praise indeed. Ideal for a summer supper, it also makes great picnic food and cuts up perfectly for nibbles with drinks.

175 g (6 oz) plain flour	**FOR THE TOPPING**
½ teaspoon salt	3 tablespoons olive oil
large pinch of cayenne pepper	450 g (1 lb) even-sized parsnips, thickly sliced
75 g (3 oz) butter	1 large leek, thickly sliced
25 g (1 oz) Parmesan, freshly grated	1 tablespoon honey
	1 tablespoon red wine vinegar
	salt and freshly ground black pepper

1. Sift the flour, salt and cayenne into a bowl and rub in the butter until the mixture resembles breadcrumbs. Stir in the Parmesan and mix to a stiff dough with 2–3 tablespoons cold water. Knead lightly, then chill the pastry while you make the topping.

2. Preheat the oven to 200°C (400°F, Gas Mark 6). Pour the oil into a deep 23 cm (9 in) flameproof gratin dish or heavy-duty cake tin and heat it on the hob. Arrange the parsnips and leek in a single layer over the surface, spoon over the honey and vinegar, then season. Cook gently for about 15 minutes, without turning or stirring the vegetables, until the parsnips are golden brown underneath and almost cooked through. Remove from the heat.

3. Roll out the pastry to a round the same diameter as the pan, carefully lift it over the vegetables and press firmly into place. Transfer the dish to the oven and bake for 20 minutes until the pastry is cooked through and golden.

4. Remove the tart from the oven and leave to stand for 5 minutes. Turn it out of the dish by placing a large serving plate on top and inverting both dish and plate, holding them firmly together, so the vegetables are on top. Serve warm or cold.

HONEY-GLAZED LEEK AND PARSNIP TART.

Spinach and Ricotta Tart

Serves 6

This tart bears little relation to the soggy quiches served in many restaurants and delicatessens. The filling is rich and fragrant and just as delicious cold or hot. I always use a deep tin for savoury tarts in order to get plenty of filling.

225 g (8 oz) shortcrust pastry, bought or home-made (see page 68)	freshly grated nutmeg
	2 eggs
	100 g (4 oz) ricotta
FOR THE FILLING	200 ml (7 fl oz) single cream
450 g (1 lb) fresh spinach, chopped, or 225 g	25 g (1 oz) Parmesan, freshly grated
(8 oz) frozen leaf spinach, thawed	25 g (1 oz) pine nuts
knob of butter	salt and freshly ground black pepper

1. Preheat the oven to 190°C (375°F, Gas Mark 5). Roll out the pastry and use to line a deep 23 cm (9 in) loose-bottomed flan tin. Line with crumpled greaseproof paper, fill with baking beans and bake for 10 minutes. Remove the paper and beans and return to the oven for a further 5 minutes.

2. If you are using fresh spinach, wash it and place it in a medium pan with only the water clinging to its leaves. Cover and cook for 3–4 minutes until tender. If you are using frozen spinach, cook it according to the packet instructions. Drain well, squeezing out any excess moisture, return the spinach to the pan with the butter, nutmeg and seasoning and mix well.

3. Beat the eggs with the ricotta and cream. Stir in the Parmesan, add to the spinach and mix well. Check the seasoning and spoon the mixture into the pastry case. Sprinkle the pine nuts over the surface and bake for 25 minutes until the filling is puffy and set. Serve warm with new potatoes and a salad.

Steamed Mushroom Pudding

Serves 6

Steamed savoury puddings with flaky suet-crust pastry are one of the joys of winter. This pud relies on the flavour of the dried mushrooms for maximum effect so don't leave them out.

225 g (8 oz) plain flour	1 large onion, finely chopped
½ teaspoon salt	1 garlic clove, crushed
2 teaspoons baking powder	680 g (1½ lb) flat mushrooms, sliced
1 teaspoon mustard powder	1 tablespoon chopped fresh thyme
2 tablespoons chopped fresh parsley	3 tablespoons chopped fresh parsley
100 g (4 oz) vegetarian suet	4 tablespoons red wine or Guinness
	1 teaspoon mushroom ketchup (optional)
FOR THE FILLING	1 teaspoon balsamic vinegar
15 g (½ oz) dried porcini mushrooms	salt and freshly ground black pepper
3 tablespoons olive oil	

1. First make the filling. Pour 150 ml (¼ pint) boiling water over the dried mushrooms and leave to soak for 15 minutes. Drain and chop them, reserving the liquid. Heat the oil in a frying pan and cook the onion and garlic for 3 minutes until softened. Add all the remaining ingredients, plus the dried mushrooms and their soaking liquid. Bring to the boil and simmer for 10 minutes, stirring occasionally, until the liquid is slightly reduced. Leave to cool.

2. To make the pastry, sift the flour with the salt, baking powder and mustard. Stir in the parsley and suet. Add about 125 ml (4 fl oz) cold water and mix to a soft dough. Turn on to a lightly floured work surface and knead lightly, then roll out to a large circle about 30–35 cm (12–14 in) in diameter. Cut out a wedge (about a quarter) and reserve for the lid. Use the remainder to line a 1.2 litre (2 pint) pudding basin.

3. Spoon the mushroom mixture into the basin. Re-roll the reserved pastry and use to make a lid, sealing the edges well. Cover the basin with greaseproof paper and foil, pleating them in the centre to allow for expansion. Tie securely with string.

4. Steam the pudding for about 1½ hours, topping the pan up with boiling water if necessary to prevent it running dry. Turn on to a warmed serving plate and serve immediately.

NON-VEGETARIAN TIP

REPLACE 450 G (1 LB) OF THE MUSHROOMS WITH AN EQUAL AMOUNT OF CUBED BRAISING STEAK AND FRY IT WITH THE ONION AND GARLIC UNTIL BROWNED. CONTINUE AS ABOVE BUT STEAM THE PUDDING FOR AN EXTRA HOUR UNTIL THE MEAT IS TENDER.

Flaky Mushroom Pie with Ginger Coriander Sauce

Serves 6

The filling for this pie is a creamy mushroom risotto mixture flavoured with fresh herbs. It can be served on its own if you don't have time to make up the whole pie.

25 g (1 oz) butter	salt and freshly ground black pepper
2 tablespoons olive oil	beaten egg to glaze
1 small onion, finely chopped	
1 garlic clove, crushed	FOR THE SAUCE
450 g (1 lb) mixed mushrooms, such as	1 shallot, finely chopped
shiitake, oyster, chestnut and flat	15 g (½ oz) butter
mushrooms, sliced	15 g (½ oz) preserved stem ginger,
150 g (5 oz) risotto rice	finely chopped
600 ml (1 pint) vegetable stock (see page 186)	4 tablespoons dry white wine
6 tablespoons chopped fresh mixed herbs, such as	1 teaspoon plain flour
tarragon, chives, basil and chervil	225 ml (8 fl oz) double cream
4 tablespoons freshly grated Parmesan	1 tablespoon chopped fresh coriander
1 amount Quick Flaky Pastry (see page 170)	1 tablespoon lemon juice

1. Preheat the oven to 200°C (400°F, Gas Mark 6). Heat the butter and oil in a heavy-based pan and cook the onion and garlic until softened. Stir in the mushrooms and continue cooking for 5 minutes until golden. Stir in the rice.

2. Heat the stock in a separate pan and simmer gently. Add a few tablespoons of the hot stock to the rice and cook, stirring constantly, until it has been absorbed. Continue to add the stock in this way until it has all been used up and the rice is just tender – it should take no more than 20 minutes. Stir in the herbs, Parmesan and seasoning, then leave to cool.

3. Roll out two-thirds of the pastry and use to line a 23 cm (9 in) loose-bottomed cake tin. Spoon the mushroom mixture in the tin and spread level. Roll out the remaining pastry and use to cover the pie, sealing the edges well. Brush with beaten egg and bake for 25–30 minutes until crisp and golden.

FLAKY MUSHROOM PIE.

4. Meanwhile, prepare the sauce. Cook the shallot in the butter until softened, then add the ginger and wine and simmer until the liquid is reduced by half. Stir in the flour and cook for 30 seconds, then add the cream. Simmer for a further 2 minutes, stirring constantly, until the sauce is smooth. Strain and pour into a clean pan. When ready to serve, gently reheat the sauce, stir in the coriander and lemon juice and season to taste. Serve with the pie.

Non-vegetarian Tip

POACH 225 G (8 OZ) SMOKED HADDOCK FILLET IN A LITTLE WATER FOR 8–10 MINUTES UNTIL JUST COOKED THROUGH. DRAIN CAREFULLY AND LEAVE TO COOL. FLAKE THE FISH AND ARRANGE IN A LAYER IN THE CENTRE OF THE PIE WITH THE RICE ABOVE AND BELOW. COOK AS DIRECTED.

Roasted Pepper and Feta Tart

Serves 4–6

You can vary the cheese used for this tart – Brie and goat's cheese are both good – and use a mixture of red and yellow peppers, if you like. If you don't want to make pastry, use 225 g (8 oz) bought pastry.

For the shortcrust pastry	For the filling
175 g (6 oz) plain flour	2 large red peppers
pinch of salt	225 g (8 oz) feta cheese, crumbled
75 g (3 oz) butter, diced	3 eggs, beaten
1 egg, beaten	300 ml (½ pint) single cream
	3 tablespoons chopped fresh chives
	salt and freshly ground black pepper

1. Preheat the oven to 200°C (400°F, Gas Mark 6). Place the peppers on a baking sheet and roast for 20 minutes until the skins are blackened. Place in a plastic bag for 5 minutes for the skins to loosen.

2. To make the pastry, sift the flour with the salt and rub in the butter until the mixture resembles breadcrumbs. Beat the egg, add to the dry ingredients and mix to a firm dough with the blade of a knife. Knead lightly on a floured surface, then wrap and chill for 15 minutes.

3. Roll out the pastry and use to line a deep 23 cm (9 in) loose-bottomed flan tin. Line with crumpled greaseproof paper, fill with baking beans and bake for 10 minutes. Remove the paper and baking beans and bake for a further 5 minutes, then remove from the oven and reduce the temperature to 180°C (350°F, Gas Mark 4). Skin and deseed the peppers and cut them into strips 5 cm (2 in) long. Arrange over the base of the tart with the cheese.

4. Beat the eggs with the cream, chives and seasoning and pour into the tart. Bake for 35–40 minutes until the filling is just set and the top is golden. Serve warm, with a green salad dressed with walnut oil.

FLAKY LEEK AND SEAWEED ROLL

Serves 6

Seaweed is not only packed with nutrients it also adds a welcome depth of flavour to meat-free cooking. This suet roll is based on a dish that came to BBC Vegetarian Good Food *magazine from TighnaMara, a vegetarian guest house situated on the shores of Loch Broom on the west coast of Scotland. It converted the magazine's editorial team to seaweed on the spot. Look out for seaweed in health-food stores and Japanese shops.*

450 g (1 lb) plain flour	*3 medium leeks, shredded*
3 teaspoons baking powder	*2 garlic cloves, chopped*
1 teaspoon salt	*100 g (4 oz) chestnut mushrooms, sliced*
175 g (6 oz) vegetarian suet	*2 tablespoons Japanese soy sauce*
150 ml (¼ pint) natural yoghurt	*2 tablespoons lemon juice*
beaten egg to glaze	*50 g (2 oz) nori or dulse seaweed, shredded*
	175 g (6 oz) carrot, grated
FOR THE FILLING	*freshly ground black pepper*
2 tablespoons olive oil	

1. Preheat the oven to 200°C (400°F, Gas Mark 6). Sift the flour, baking powder and salt into a bowl and stir in the suet. Mix the yoghurt with 150 ml (¼ pint) water and add to the dry ingredients. Mix to a firm dough and knead lightly on a floured surface. Cover and set aside.

2. To make the filling, heat the oil in a frying pan and cook the leeks and garlic for 5 minutes until softened. Add the mushrooms and cook for a further 2 minutes, then stir in all the remaining ingredients. Leave to cool.

3. Roll out the dough on a lightly floured surface to a 30 x 40 cm (12 x 16 in) rectangle. Spread the filling over the dough and roll up from one end. Place on a greased baking sheet, brush with beaten egg and cook for 40–45 minutes until puffy and golden. Serve cut into slices, with Onion Gravy (see page 184) and mashed celeriac.

Asparagus, Red Pepper and Goat's Cheese Slice

Serves 6

*If you prefer you can use 450 g (1 lb) frozen puff pastry
or filo instead of making shortcrust.*

225 g (8 oz) plain flour	225 g (8 oz) asparagus spears
pinch of salt	1 tablespoon olive oil
¼ teaspoon mustard powder	1 shallot or small onion, chopped
100 g (4 oz) butter, diced	1 garlic clove, crushed
50 g (2 oz) Cheddar, grated	350 g (12 oz) fresh spinach, blanched or 225 g
1 egg yolk	(8 oz) frozen spinach, thawed
beaten egg to glaze	2 tablespoons crème fraîche
2 teaspoons sesame seeds	25 g (1 oz) pine nuts
	100 g (4 oz) firm goat's cheese, crumbled
FOR THE FILLING	salt and freshly ground black pepper
2 red peppers	

1. To make the pastry, sift the flour, salt and mustard into a bowl and rub in the butter until the mixture resembles breadcrumbs. Stir in the cheese. Mix the egg yolk with 2 tablespoons cold water and sprinkle it over the dry ingredients, then mix to a firm dough. Knead lightly, then wrap and chill for 15 minutes while you prepare the filling.

2. Grill the peppers on all sides until blackened, then place in a plastic bag and leave for 5 minutes for the skins to soften. Peel off the skins, deseed the peppers and cut into 5 cm (2 in) strips. Cook the asparagus spears in boiling water for 8–10 minutes until tender, then drain and leave to cool.

3. Preheat the oven to 190°C (375°F, Gas Mark 5). Heat the oil in a pan and cook the shallot or onion and garlic until softened. Squeeze the spinach dry and chop roughly. Stir it into the onion with the crème fraîche, pine nuts and seasoning, then leave to cool.

4. Roll out the pastry to a 30 cm (12 in) square. Arrange the spinach mixture down the centre to form a block about 13 cm (5 in) wide. Arrange the asparagus spears on top, then scatter over the goat's cheese. Place the pepper strips on top of the cheese.

Asparagus, Red Pepper and Goat's Cheese Slice with Quick Lemon Hollandaise (see page 187) and French Beans with Roasted Almonds (see page 120).

5. Brush the pastry edges with water and make diagonal cuts up to the filling about 2.5 cm (1 in) wide. Fold these strips over the filling, alternating from each side, to form a parcel. Place on a baking sheet, brush with beaten egg and scatter over the sesame seeds. Bake for 25–30 minutes until golden. Serve hot or cold, cut into slices.

GRUYÈRE AND RED ONION GOUGÈRE

Serves 4 as a light supper

Serve this light, cheesy pastry thinly sliced as a pre-dinner nibble, cut in wedges with a green salad for a simple starter or supper dish, or filled with sautéed mushrooms for a more substantial meal.

100 g (4 oz) plain flour	*100 g (4 oz) Gruyère cheese, diced*
1 teaspoon salt	*1 red onion, finely chopped*
¼ teaspoon cayenne pepper	*1 tablespoon chopped fresh tarragon (optional)*
100 g (4 oz) butter, diced	*2 tablespoons freshly grated Parmesan*
4 eggs, beaten	

1. Preheat the oven to 220°C (425°F, Gas Mark 7). Sift the flour, salt and cayenne on to a sheet of kitchen paper or greaseproof paper. Place the butter in a pan with 150 ml (¼ pint) water and bring slowly to the boil. Quickly tip in the flour all at once and beat well. Remove the pan from the heat and continue to beat until the mixture leaves the sides of the pan (this can be done with an electric hand-held mixer). Leave until the dough is cool to the touch, then beat in the eggs a spoonful at a time, making sure each addition is thoroughly absorbed before beating in the next. The dough should be stiff and glossy; you may not need to add all the egg.

2. Stir in the Gruyère, onion and tarragon, if using. Spoon the mixture on to a greased baking sheet and shape into a 20 cm (8 in) circle. Scoop out the centre so that the gougère has a thick border but is thin in the centre. Sprinkle with the Parmesan cheese.

3. Bake for 25–30 minutes until well risen and golden and then serve at once, cut into slices.

WILD MUSHROOM AND LEEK CROUSTADES

Serves 4

My sister-in-law, Debbie, is an inspirational cook whose ideas for meat-free dishes are always both stylish and tasty. This recipe is based on one of her ideas. Prepare all the elements ahead, then reheat the pastry squares and warm through the mushroom mixture just before serving.

450 g (1 lb) puff pastry, thawed if frozen	350 g (12 oz) mixed wild mushrooms, such as
beaten egg to glaze	chanterelle, shiitake, oyster and flat mushrooms,
1 teaspoon sesame seeds	cut in half if large
	2 tablespoons Madeira
FOR THE FILLING	1 teaspoon Dijon mustard
15 g (½ oz) dried porcini mushrooms	3 tablespoons chopped fresh parsley
3 tablespoons olive oil	4 tablespoons crème fraîche
2 garlic cloves, crushed	salt and freshly ground black pepper
3 leeks, shredded	fresh herb sprigs to garnish

1. Preheat the oven to 220°C (425°F, Gas Mark 7). Soak the dried mushrooms in 150 ml (¼ pint) boiling water for 15 minutes. Drain, reserving the liquid, and chop the mushrooms.

2. Roll out the pastry to 3 mm (⅛ in) thick and cut it into eight 13 cm (5 in) squares. Arrange on dampened baking sheets and lightly score half the squares with a knife to form a lattice pattern. Brush these four with beaten egg and sprinkle with the sesame seeds. Bake all the pastry squares for 10–15 minutes until puffy and golden.

3. Meanwhile, heat the oil in a frying pan, add the garlic and leeks and cook gently over a low heat for 10 minutes until really soft and golden. Add the dried and fresh mushrooms and cook for 5 minutes, then add the Madeira. Heat for 30 seconds, then stir in the mustard, seasoning and reserved liquid from the mushrooms and simmer for 5–10 minutes until the liquid has almost evaporated. Stir in the parsley and crème fraîche and simmer until thickened. Check the seasoning.

4. To assemble, arrange the unglazed pastry squares on warm serving plates and spoon the mushroom mixture over them. Arrange the remaining pastry squares on top and garnish with fresh herb sprigs.

ONION TART WITH BLACK OLIVE PASTRY

Serves 6

I've been making this tart for summer lunches and to take on picnics for years and never varied from the basic recipe until recently, when I read about an olive pastry that I felt would go well with the filling. I tried it and it did, so here it is!

175 g (6 oz) plain flour	*FOR THE FILLING*
pinch of salt	*25 g (1 oz) butter*
75 g (3 oz) butter, diced	*2 tablespoons olive oil*
25 g (1 oz) stoned black olives, finely chopped	*680 g (1½ lb) onions, sliced*
1 egg, beaten	*4 egg yolks*
	200 ml (7 fl oz) double cream
	freshly grated nutmeg
	salt and freshly ground black pepper

1. Preheat the oven to 200°C (400°F, Gas Mark 6). Sift the flour and salt into a mixing bowl and rub in the butter until the mixture resembles breadcrumbs. Stir in the olives, then add the egg and mix to a soft dough with the blade of a knife. Knead lightly on a floured work surface, then wrap and chill for 15 minutes.

2. Meanwhile, prepare the filling. Heat the butter and oil in a frying pan, add the onions and cook over a low heat for 30 minutes, stirring occasionally, until pale golden. Season with salt, pepper and nutmeg and remove from the heat. Beat the egg yolks with the cream and stir into the onions.

3. Roll out the pastry and use to line a deep 23 cm (9 in) loose-bottomed flan tin. Line with crumpled greaseproof paper, fill with baking beans and bake for 10 minutes. Remove the paper and beans and return the pastry case to the oven for a further 5 minutes.

4. Place the flan tin on a baking sheet, pour in the filling and level the top. Bake for 30 minutes until the filling is set and golden. Serve warm.

Harvest Plate Pie

Serves 4

I love old-fashioned plate pies but tend to make them with sweet fillings: blackberry in the autumn, fresh raspberry in the summer and, of course, mincemeat for Christmas. This is a savoury version and I often serve it for a family Sunday lunch with creamy mashed potatoes and runner beans.

450 g (1 lb) puff pastry, thawed if frozen	1 large potato, cubed
beaten egg to glaze	100 g (4 oz) sweetcorn, thawed if frozen
	25 g (1 oz) butter
FOR THE FILLING	25 g (1 oz) plain flour
2 tablespoons olive oil	50 g (2 oz) Cheddar, grated
2 medium leeks, sliced	3 tablespoons chopped fresh chives
1 medium onion, sliced	salt and freshly ground black pepper
2 medium carrots, sliced	

1. Preheat the oven to 220°C (425°F, Gas Mark 7). Heat the oil in a frying pan, add the leeks and onion and cook for 5 minutes until softened. Add the carrots and potato with 300 ml (½ pint) water, bring to the boil and simmer for 5 minutes until the vegetables are almost tender. Drain, reserving the cooking liquid, then mix the vegetables with the sweetcorn.

2. Melt the butter in a small pan, stir in the flour and cook for 1 minute. Gradually add the reserved cooking liquid and cook, stirring, until it forms a thick sauce. Simmer for 3 minutes, stirring often, then remove from the heat and stir in the cheese, chives and seasoning. Pour the sauce over the vegetables and leave to cool.

3. Roll out half the pastry and use to line a 20 cm (8 in) pie plate. Spoon the vegetable mixture into the pastry, leaving a 2.5 cm (1 in) border. Brush the edges with water. Roll out the rest of the pastry and use to cover the pie. Trim the edges neatly and pinch together to seal.

4. Place the pie plate on a baking sheet, make a steam hole in the middle of the pastry lid and decorate with the pastry trimmings. Brush with beaten egg and bake for 25–30 minutes until the pastry is puffy and golden. Serve immediately.

Non-vegetarian Tip

CUT A 225 G (8 OZ) GAMMON STEAK INTO STRIPS AND FRY WITH THE LEEKS AND ONION. CONTINUE AS ABOVE.

Spiced Carrot and Coriander Strudel

Serves 4

This is a little like a large spring roll but with a Thai spiced filling. Serve it with
Spicy Peanut Sauce (see page 185).

10 large sheets filo pastry	*1 red chilli, seeded and chopped*
4 teaspoons sesame oil	*225 g (8 oz) oyster mushrooms, sliced*
2 tablespoons sunflower oil	*3 medium carrots, grated*
	50g (2oz) bean sprouts
For the filling	*50 g (2oz) unsalted peanuts, chopped*
2 tablespoons sunflower oil	*3 tablespoons chopped fresh coriander*
1 small onion, finely chopped	*2 medium tomatoes, skinned, seeded and chopped*
1 garlic clove, crushed	*2 tablespoons Kikkoman soy sauce*
1 teaspoon grated fresh root ginger	*salt and freshly ground black pepper*
½ stick lemon grass, chopped	

1. Preheat the oven to 220°C (425°F, Gas Mark 7). To make the filling, heat the oil in a medium pan, add the onion and garlic and cook for 3 minutes until softened. Stir in the ginger, lemon grass and chilli and cook for a further 2 minutes. Add the mushrooms, carrots, bean sprouts, peanuts, coriander and tomatoes and mix well. Season to taste.

2. Mix 1 teaspoon of the sesame oil with the sunflower oil. Lay out the filo sheets, overlapping the edges, to form a large square about 50 cm (20 in), trimming if necessary. Brush each sheet with the sesame and sunflower oil mixture. Cover the top two-thirds of the pastry with the filling, leaving a 2.5 cm (1 in) border. Sprinkle with the soy sauce.

3. Carefully roll up the strudel from the top edge, then transfer to a greased baking sheet, curving it to fit if necessary. Brush with the remaining sesame oil, bake for 20–25 minutes until golden and then serve.

Vegetables

*H*OW CAN ANYONE consider a vegetarian diet dull when faced with the enormous range of tastes, textures and colours offered by wonderful fresh vegetables? Brown and boring are the last words that come to mind when looking at what's on offer in any top-quality greengrocer's – the average butcher simply cannot compete. And why do you think supermarkets always place the fresh fruit and vegetable section at the entrance to their stores? The choice of fresh vegetables, both familiar and exotic, is increasing all the time and each newcomer stocked by supermarkets and greengrocers provides further scope for the adventurous cook.

The quality of the basic ingredients is supremely important when making a vegetable-based dish so I would suggest buying organic if you can find a good supplier. Supermarkets have jumped on the organic bandwagon but their supplies are somewhat limited and erratic. Try to find out if there is a vegetable box scheme in your area which will deliver a regular supply to you at home. Schemes vary, so contact the Soil Association for information.

I realize that for many people a daily shop for fresh vegetables is a near impossibility, but your cooking will taste far better and have greater nutritional value if you use fresh produce as soon as possible after buying it. Try to plan accordingly and use up odds and ends in soups and stocks.

WINTER VEGETABLE STEW WITH LEEK DUMPLINGS

This stew can be served without the dumplings but it will not be nearly as interesting!
Surprisingly, Worcestershire sauce is not suitable for vegetarians as it contains anchovies,
but a vegetarian version can be obtained from health-food shops.

4 tablespoons olive oil	*1 tablespoon Worcestershire sauce*
1 garlic clove, crushed	*2 bay leaves*
350 g (12 oz) shallots or button onions, peeled	*1 bouquet garni*
(see page 37)	*2 tablespoons tomato purée*
2 celery sticks, sliced	*salt and freshly ground black pepper*
2 large carrots, sliced	
2 large parsnips, sliced	*FOR THE DUMPLINGS*
225 g (8 oz) pumpkin flesh, cut into chunks	*1 teaspoon sunflower oil*
1 tablespoon plain flour	*1 small leek, finely sliced*
2 tablespoons chopped fresh parsley	*100 g (4 oz) self-raising flour*
300 ml (½ pint) vegetable stock (see page 186)	*40 g (1½ oz) vegetarian suet*
250 ml (9 fl oz) can Guinness	*4–5 tablespoons milk or water*

1. Preheat the oven to 180°C (350°F, Gas Mark 4). Heat the oil in a large ovenproof casserole, add the garlic, shallots or button onions and celery and fry over a medium-high heat for 5 minutes until golden. Add the rest of the vegetables and fry until lightly browned. Sprinkle over the flour and stir in.

2. Stir in all the remaining ingredients, season well and bring to the boil, stirring. Transfer to the oven and bake for 20 minutes.

3. Meanwhile, make the dumplings. Heat the oil in a small pan and cook the leek until softened. Sift the flour into a bowl with plenty of seasoning and stir in the suet, followed by the leek. Bind to a firm dough with the milk or water and, with floured hands, roll the mixture into 12 small balls.

4. Remove the casserole from the oven and stir well. Arrange the dumplings over the surface and return to the oven, uncovered, for 20–25 minutes until the dumplings are light and fluffy. Serve immediately with mashed potatoes.

WINTER VEGETABLE STEW WITH LEEK DUMPLINGS.

Celeriac and Broccoli Bake with Sesame Crumb Topping

Serves 4

Look in the chiller cabinet of your local supermarket and you are likely to find a cheesy vegetable dish, alongside the vegetable lasagne. Most vegetarians must be heartily sick of both, since they are served up again and again as the only 'veggie alternative'. Both can be quite inedible when prepared commercially which is a pity, as with a little care and the freshest ingredients they should be delicious. This is my version of the former.

225 g (8 oz) celeriac, cubed	*100 g (4 oz) Cheddar, grated*
225 g (8 oz) broccoli, cut into florets	*225 g (8 oz) chestnut mushrooms, sliced*
50 g (2 oz) butter	*100 g (4 oz) sweetcorn*
40 g (1½ oz) plain flour	*75 g (3 oz) fresh wholemeal breadcrumbs*
450 ml (¾ pint) semi-skimmed milk	*25 g (1 oz) sesame seeds*
150 ml (¼ pint) hot vegetable stock	*pinch of cayenne pepper*
(see page 186)	*salt and freshly ground black pepper*

1. Preheat the oven to 200°C (400°F, Gas Mark 6). Place the celeriac in a large pan of water, bring to the boil and simmer for 10 minutes until just tender. Add the broccoli for the last 2 minutes. Drain thoroughly.

2. Meanwhile, melt 40 g (1½ oz) of the butter in a medium pan, add the flour and cook for 1 minute, stirring. Remove from the heat and gradually whisk in the milk and stock, then return the pan to the heat and cook, stirring, until the sauce thickens and comes to the boil.

3. Remove the sauce from the heat and stir in two-thirds of the cheese. Season to taste, then add the celeriac, broccoli, mushrooms and sweetcorn.

4. Transfer the mixture to a large shallow gratin dish. Mix together the breadcrumbs, sesame seeds, cayenne and seasoning and scatter over the top of the vegetables. Dot with the remaining butter and bake for 15–20 minutes until the top is golden. Serve immediately.

BAKED ROOTS WITH GOAT'S CHEESE

Serves 4

Root vegetables combine extremely well with cheese, and this simple bake makes an ideal dish to serve to friends on a cold night. I sometimes cook it in individual gratin dishes if I'm in a hurry, as this means the cooking time can be reduced by about 20 minutes.

225 g (8 oz) potatoes	150 ml (¼ pint) double cream
225 g (8 oz) swede	150 ml (¼ pint) milk
225 g (8 oz) celeriac	freshly grated nutmeg
225 g (8 oz) parsnips	15 g (½ oz) butter
2 leeks, thinly sliced	salt and freshly ground black pepper
175 g (6 oz) goat's cheese, crumbled	

1. Preheat the oven to 170°C (325°F, Gas Mark 3). Peel the root vegetables and cut them into matchsticks 6 cm (2½ in) long. Mix them with the leeks, goat's cheese and plenty of seasoning, then tip into a buttered gratin dish or roasting tin and level the surface.

2. Mix the cream with the milk, nutmeg and seasoning and pour it over the vegetables. Dot the top with the butter and cook for 50–60 minutes until the vegetables are tender. Cover the top with foil if it browns too quickly. Serve with broccoli or green beans.

RED PEPPERS WITH PESTO RISOTTO

Serves 4

Ready-made pesto sauce has improved dramatically over the past few years but most contain Parmesan made with animal rennet. There are some vegetarian versions available, however, or you could make your own (see page 188) and freeze it.

4 large red peppers, halved and seeded	1 litre (1¾ pints) vegetable stock
3 tablespoons olive oil	(see page 186)
1 onion, finely chopped	3 tablespoons pesto sauce
1 garlic clove, chopped	25 g (1 oz) pine nuts
175 g (6 oz) risotto rice	4 tablespoons freshly grated Parmesan
	salt and freshly ground black pepper

1. Preheat the oven to 180°C (350°F, Gas Mark 4). Brush the pepper halves inside and out with a little of the olive oil and bake for 10 minutes, until just softened. Keep warm.

2. Meanwhile, heat the remaining oil in a medium pan and cook the onion and garlic for 3 minutes until softened. Add the rice and stir for 1 minute to coat it with the oil.

3. Heat the stock in a separate pan until simmering. Add 150 ml (¼ pint) stock to the rice and simmer, stirring constantly, until absorbed. Continue adding the stock a little at a time, stirring until it has been absorbed before adding the next lot, until the rice is just tender and all the stock used up – this should take about 20 minutes and the risotto should be creamy. Stir in the pesto sauce and season to taste.

4. Pile the rice into the pepper halves, sprinkle with the pine nuts and Parmesan and place briefly under a hot grill to toast the nuts. Serve immediately with a leafy salad and Italian bread.

RED PEPPERS WITH PESTO RISOTTO.

HONEY-GLAZED VEGETABLE KEBABS
WITH ONION RELISH

Serves 4

Root vegetables are so much more versatile than many people realize – they are particularly good served together as the different flavours seem to enhance each other. This is a winter dish but I often use the same glaze with new potatoes for summer barbecues.

680 g (1½lb) mixed root vegetables, such as	FOR THE ONION RELISH
celeriac, parsnip, swede, carrots, etc.,	1 tablespoon olive oil
cut into 5 cm (2 in) cubes	2 large onions, finely sliced
2 tablespoons clear honey	4 tablespoons white wine vinegar
1 teaspoon ground cumin	4 tablespoons light muscovado sugar
1 garlic clove, crushed	50 g (2 oz) raisins
2 tablespoons olive oil	1 teaspoon mustard seeds
salt and freshly ground black pepper	

1. Bring a medium pan of water to the boil, add the vegetables and cook for 5 minutes, then drain and refresh under cold running water.

2. Mix the honey, cumin, garlic, olive oil and seasoning together in a small bowl. Thread the vegetable cubes on to skewers and brush with the honey glaze.

3. To make the onion relish, heat the oil in a small pan over a low heat, add the onions and cook for 5 minutes until softened but not browned. Add all the remaining ingredients and simmer, stirring occasionally, for 10 minutes until the liquid has evaporated and the onions are really soft.

4. While the relish is cooking, preheat the grill. Grill the kebabs for 20–25 minutes until golden and tender, brushing with the glaze several times and turning occasionally. Serve with the onion relish and some steamed rice.

NON-VEGETARIAN TIP

HALVE THE AMOUNT OF VEGETABLES AND ADD 350 G (12 OZ) BONELESS SKINLESS CHICKEN, CUT INTO 5 CM (2 IN) CUBES. COOK THE VEGETABLES IN BOILING WATER FOR 8 MINUTES. THREAD THEM ON TO SKEWERS WITH THE CHICKEN AND GRILL OR BARBECUE FOR 15–20 MINUTES, BRUSHING WITH THE GLAZE AS INSTRUCTED.

Roasted Root Vegetables with Cranberry Orange Sauce

Serves 4

In this recipe the technique of roasting in olive oil is applied to homely English root vegetables and the result makes a really satisfying winter meal. I regularly serve this dish with Yorkshire pudding and horseradish cream sauce for a traditional Sunday lunch. Use any roots you have available.

1 medium swede, about 225 g (8 oz)	1 tablespoon sesame seeds
1 medium sweet potato	salt and freshly ground black pepper
2 medium parsnips	
3 small carrots	FOR THE SAUCE
225 g (8 oz) medium new potatoes	100 g (4 oz) fresh cranberries
6 tablespoons olive oil	50 g (2 oz) granulated sugar
2 sprigs of fresh rosemary	grated rind and juice of ½ orange
12 shallots or button onions, peeled	1 tablespoon lemon juice
8 garlic cloves, unpeeled	2 tablespoons port (optional)

1. Preheat the oven to 220°C (425°F, Gas Mark 7). Peel the swede, sweet potato and parsnips and cut them into large chunks. Scrub the carrots and new potatoes and cut them in half. Bring two large pans of water to the boil, put the sweet potato and swede into one and the parsnips, carrots and new potatoes into the other. Return to the boil and simmer for 5 minutes, then drain thoroughly.

2. Put the olive oil into a large roasting tin and place it in the oven for 5 minutes until very hot. Remove and add the root vegetables to the oil, basting well. Season and add the rosemary sprigs. Roast for 25 minutes, then remove the pan from the oven and turn the vegetables. Add the shallots, garlic and sesame seeds and return to the oven for a further 20–25 minutes until the vegetables are golden.

3. While the vegetables are cooking, make the sauce. Place the cranberries in a small pan with the sugar, orange rind and juice and lemon juice. Add the port, if using. Cook over a gentle heat for 5–10 minutes until the cranberries have softened and formed a thick sauce. Serve with the roasted vegetables.

Non-vegetarian Tip

THESE ROASTED VEGETABLES MAKE AN EXCELLENT ACCOMPANIMENT TO ANY TRADITIONAL ROAST OR GRILLED MEAT.

CAULIFLOWER AND GREEN BEAN KORMA

I like mild, creamy sauces for curries so korma is one of my favourites. Balance it with a sharp, acidic vegetable dish such as Chick Pea and Lentil Curry (see page 104), add a rice pilaff and some fresh chutneys and you have a colourful and tasty meal. Ground cashew nuts give this mild sauce its creamy texture and distinctive flavour but you can use blanched almonds instead.

2 medium onions	¼ teaspoon ground cinnamon
2.5 cm (1 in) piece fresh root ginger, roughly chopped	¼ teaspoon ground cardamom
1 large garlic clove	1 teaspoon salt
50 g (2 oz) unsalted cashew nuts	1 medium cauliflower, divided into florets
1–2 red chillies	175 g (6 oz) French beans, halved
2 tablespoons sunflower oil	2 medium carrots, thickly sliced
1 teaspoon ground coriander	100 g (4 oz) yoghurt
½ teaspoon ground cumin	fresh coriander leaves and toasted cashew nuts to garnish

1. Halve the onions, cut one half into chunks and thinly slice the rest. Place the chunks of onion in a blender with the ginger, garlic, cashew nuts and chillies, add 6 tablespoons water and process until smooth.

2. Heat the oil in a large heavy-based pan and add the sliced onion. Fry over a medium heat for 6–8 minutes, stirring frequently, until golden. Stir in the spices and cook for 1 minute. Add the contents of the blender and continue frying until the oil starts to separate from the mixture.

3. Wash out the blender goblet with 150 ml (¼ pint) water and add to the pan with the salt, then add the vegetables. Stir in the yoghurt a tablespoonful at a time, mix well, then cover and simmer for about 20 minutes until the vegetables are tender, stirring occasionally.

4. Transfer the korma to a warmed serving dish, garnish with fresh coriander leaves and toasted cashews and serve with basmati rice.

NON-VEGETARIAN TIP

AFTER COOKING THE SPICES, ADD 350 G (12 OZ) SKINLESS, BONELESS CHICKEN BREASTS, CUT INTO 5 CM (2 IN) STRIPS. CONTINUE AS ABOVE BUT ADD ONLY HALF THE AMOUNT OF VEGETABLES.

Celeriac, Potato and Leek Gratin

Serves 4

Served in large earthenware dishes, gratins are wonderful for parties – warm and filling, they satisfy meat eaters and vegetarians alike. This version is inspired by the Scandinavian dish known as Janssen's Temptation. The original is made with potatoes, onions, anchovies and cream; I've used leeks instead of onion, omitted the anchovies and come up with a dish that is just the thing to withstand those sub-zero temperatures.

1 tablespoon olive oil	*450 g (1 lb) celeriac, cut into matchsticks*
knob of butter	*150 ml (¼ pint) double cream*
350 g (12 oz) leeks, thinly sliced	*150 ml (¼ pint) milk*
680 g (1½ lb) potatoes, cut into matchsticks	*salt and freshly ground black pepper*

1. Preheat the oven to 200°C (400°F, Gas Mark 6). Heat the oil and butter in a frying pan, add the leeks and cook gently for 5 minutes until softened. Mix with the potatoes, celeriac and plenty of seasoning.

2. Transfer the vegetables to a buttered large shallow baking dish. Mix the cream and milk together and pour on to the vegetables. Bake for 1 hour until the vegetables are tender. Cover with foil if the top browns too quickly. Serve immediately.

Non-vegetarian Tip

ADD 6 CHOPPED ANCHOVY FILLETS TO THE VEGETABLE MIXTURE BEFORE BAKING; SERVE WITH VENISON OR LAMB SAUSAGES.

SPICED VEGETABLE RAGOUT WITH COUSCOUS

Serves 4

If you can't get couscous, serve this vegetable ragout with wholegrain basmati rice.
Harissa is a pungent spice paste used in North African cookery and available
from some delicatessens.

275 g (10 oz) couscous	*½ teaspoon ground cinnamon*
2 tablespoons olive oil	*100 g (4 oz) baby carrots*
pinch of ground cloves	*100 g (4 oz) baby turnips*
2 tablespoons chopped fresh coriander	*300 ml (½ pint) vegetable stock*
	(see page 186)
FOR THE VEGETABLE RAGOUT	*1 teaspoon tomato purée*
2 tablespoons olive oil	*225 g (8 oz) French beans, halved*
1 large red onion, sliced	*225 g (8 oz) courgettes, sliced on the diagonal*
2 garlic cloves, chopped	*425 g (15 oz) can chick peas, drained*
1 teaspoon paprika	*1–2 teaspoons chilli sauce or harissa*
1 teaspoon ground ginger	*salt and freshly ground black pepper*

1. First make the ragout. Heat the oil in a flameproof casserole, add the onion and garlic and cook for 3 minutes until softened. Stir in the spices and cook for 1 minute, then add the carrots and turnips, stock, tomato purée and seasoning. Bring to the boil and simmer for 10 minutes, then add the French beans, courgettes and chick peas. Simmer for a further 5 minutes, then stir in the chilli sauce or harissa.

2. Place the couscous in a bowl, pour over 300 ml (½ pint) cold water and stir gently to mix. Leave to soak for 15 minutes, stirring occasionally to break up any lumps.

3. Heat the oil in a medium pan, add the couscous, cloves and seasoning and heat through gently until the grains are separate and dry. Spoon into a serving dish, arrange the ragout on top and garnish with the chopped coriander.

NON-VEGETARIAN TIP

THIS DISH GOES WELL WITH ANY KIND OF ROAST OR GRILLED LAMB.

Parsnip and Walnut Roulade

Serves 4

*This cheesy roll is excellent both hot and cold. Serve it cut into thick slices,
with seasonal vegetables.*

350 g (12 oz) parsnips, sliced	*FOR THE FILLING*
15 g (½ oz) butter	*25 g (1 oz) butter*
1 tablespoon plain flour	*1 medium onion, sliced*
4 eggs, separated	*1 tablespoon plain flour*
25 g (1 oz) walnut pieces, toasted and chopped	*150 ml (¼ pint) semi-skimmed milk*
pinch of cayenne pepper	*75 g (3 oz) Stilton cheese, crumbled*
3 tablespoons freshly grated Parmesan	*1 small bunch watercress, leaves*
salt and freshly ground black pepper	*finely chopped*

1. Preheat the oven to 190°C (375°F, Gas Mark 5). Cook the parsnips in boiling water for about 15 minutes until tender and then drain thoroughly. Purée in a blender or food processor until smooth.

2. Melt the butter in a medium pan, stir in the flour and cook for 1 minute. Beat in the parsnip purée and the egg yolks, then remove from the heat and season well. Stir in the walnuts and cayenne. Whisk the egg whites until stiff and carefully fold them into the parsnip mixture.

3. Pour the mixture into a greased and lined 20 x 30 cm (8 x 12 in) Swiss roll tin, smooth the surface and scatter the Parmesan cheese over the top. Bake for 15 minutes until golden and firm to the touch.

4. While the roulade is cooking, make the filling. Melt the butter in a medium pan and cook the onion over a low heat for 10 minutes until soft and golden. Stir in the flour and cook for 1 minute. Remove from the heat and gradually whisk in the milk, then return to the heat and bring to the boil, stirring constantly, until the sauce is thick and smooth. Remove from the heat again and stir in the Stilton, watercress and seasoning to taste.

5. Turn the roulade out on to a sheet of baking parchment, peel off the lining paper and spread with the filling. Roll up carefully from a short end, using the baking parchment to help support the roll. Transfer to a warmed serving dish and serve immediately.

Hazelnut, Leek and Mushroom Terrine

Serves 4–6

I make this versatile terrine for picnics and summer parties as it travels well and tastes wonderful. Lining the terrine with blanched leeks is not difficult to do but gives it an attractive finish.

3 large leeks	75 g (3 oz) fresh brown breadcrumbs
7g (¼ oz) dried porcini mushrooms	50 g (2 oz) toasted hazelnuts, finely chopped
2 tablespoons olive oil	100 g (4 oz) Cheshire cheese, grated
1 large onion, chopped	1 egg, beaten
2 garlic cloves, chopped	3 tablespoons chopped fresh basil
450 g (1 lb) chestnut mushrooms, finely chopped	2 tablespoons chopped fresh thyme
	salt and freshly ground black pepper
225 g (8 oz) carrots, grated	

1. Cut the leeks in half lengthways and blanch in boiling water for 30 seconds. Drain and refresh under cold running water. Pat dry, separate the layers and use to line the base and sides of an oiled 23 x 13 cm (9 x 5 in) loaf tin, making sure there are no gaps and leaving the edges of the leeks overhanging the sides of the tin. Soak the porcini in 4 tablespoons boiling water, then drain and chop.

2. Preheat the oven to 170°C (325°F, Gas Mark 3). Heat the oil in a large frying pan and cook the onion and garlic for 3 minutes until softened. Add the chestnut mushrooms and chopped porcini and cook for a further 5 minutes. Place all the remaining ingredients in a large bowl, add the mushroom mixture and stir until thoroughly combined. Spoon into the lined tin and press down lightly. Fold over the leeks to cover the filling.

3. Cover the tin tightly with foil and bake for 1¼ to 1½ hours until the terrine feels firm in the centre. Leave to cool for 5 minutes in the tin, then turn it out and slice if serving hot. If serving cold, cool in the tin completely and chill before slicing. Serve the terrine with new potatoes and salad.

Vegetable Parcels with Saffron Butter

Serves 4

I find many of the baby vegetables now available all year round somewhat tasteless. Marketed for size and tenderness, they lose out on flavour when compared to the young vegetables I get from my local pick-your-own farm. So I only make this dish in the late spring, when English-grown vegetables are appearing in the shops. During winter the recipe works well with root vegetables, blanched, cubed and tossed in olive oil and rosemary.

680 g (1½ lb) baby vegetables, such as new potatoes, courgettes, French beans, asparagus tips, carrots and cauliflower florets	*75 g (3 oz) butter*
	4 tablespoons chopped fresh herbs, such as basil, chives, chervil and tarragon
50 g (2 oz) pine nuts, toasted	*salt and freshly ground black pepper*
¼ teaspoon saffron strands	

1. Preheat the oven to 200°C (400°F, Gas Mark 6). Cut four baking parchment circles, 30 cm (12 in) in diameter, and make a crease down the centre of each one. Trim the vegetables and cut up any larger ones so they are all the same size. Mix with the pine nuts.

2. Place the saffron strands in a small pan and cook for 30 seconds until golden. Crush them between two teaspoons, then place in a bowl with the butter and beat until softened. Beat in the herbs and seasoning.

3. Divide the vegetables and pine nuts between the paper circles, putting them to one side of the crease, and top with the butter. Fold over the paper to enclose the vegetables and then turn in the edges to seal. Place on a baking sheet and cook for 25–30 minutes until tender. Serve the vegetable parcels with the paper just opened, accompanied by steamed rice or pasta.

Baked Field Mushrooms with an Olive Crust

Serves 4

Great big flat mushrooms are about the only vegetable that I can be bothered to stuff, since they don't need to be hollowed out. Serve these on a bed of risotto rice mixed with grated mozzarella and shredded fresh basil.

8 large flat field mushrooms	*25 g (1 oz) fresh white breadcrumbs*
3 tablespoons olive oil	*1 garlic clove, chopped*
	2 tablespoons chopped fresh parsley
FOR THE OLIVE CRUST	*1 tablespoon chopped fresh chives*
50 g (2 oz) stoned black olives, finely chopped	*2 tablespoons freshly grated Parmesan*
25 g (1 oz) shelled pistachio nuts or almonds, finely chopped	*salt and freshly ground black pepper*

1. Preheat the oven to 200°C (400°F, Gas Mark 6). Remove the stalks from the mushrooms, set the caps aside and finely chop the stalks. Mix with all the stuffing ingredients and season well.

2. Arrange the mushroom caps on an oiled baking sheet and spoon the olive mixture into the centre of each one. Level the surface and drizzle with the olive oil. Bake for 15–20 minutes and then serve immediately.

Baked Butternut Squash with Chilli and Lime Butter

Serves 2

Butternut squash has a hard golden skin and resembles a large pear in shape. Its firm, sweet flesh is wonderful when baked simply as in this recipe. Serve with crusty bread and a salad of bitter leaves for an uncomplicated yet satisfying meal.

1 butternut squash, about 680 g (1½ lb)	*1 small red chilli, seeded and chopped*
50 g (2 oz) softened butter	*2 tablespoons chopped fresh coriander*
grated rind and juice of 1 lime	*salt and freshly ground black pepper*

1. Preheat the oven to 180°C (350°F, Gas Mark 4). Place the whole squash in a large pan of water, bring to the boil and simmer for 10 minutes. Drain and cut the squash in half lengthways. Scoop out the seeds and discard. Place the squash, cut-sides up, in a roasting tin.

2. Beat the butter with the lime rind and juice, chilli, coriander and seasoning. Spread over the cut surfaces of the squash and bake for 15 minutes until tender and golden. Serve immediately.

LEEK AND ONION YORKSHIRE PUDDING

Serves 4

Just because you don't eat beef, there is absolutely no reason to give up one of life's great treats – Yorkshire pudding. This recipe is half way between a Yorkshire pud and toad-in-the-hole, but made with richly flavoured caramelized vegetables instead of meat. It can also be made in twelve tartlet tins to make mini puddings. Serve it with Roasted Root Vegetables (see page 85) and Onion Gravy (see page 184) for the greatest effect.

3 tablespoons olive oil	FOR THE BATTER
450 g (1 lb) shallots or button onions, peeled	*100 g (4 oz) plain flour*
(see page 37)	*pinch of salt*
2 leeks, thickly sliced	*¼ teaspoon mustard powder*
1 tablespoon granulated sugar	*1 egg, beaten*
	300 ml (½ pint) semi-skimmed milk and
	water mixed

1. Preheat the oven to 220°C (425°F, Gas Mark 7). Pour the oil into a small heavy-duty roasting tin and put in the oven until very hot. Add the shallots or button onions and leeks and sprinkle with the sugar. Cook on the hob over a medium heat for 10–15 minutes until golden brown.

2. Meanwhile, make the batter. Sift the flour, salt and mustard into a mixing bowl and make a well in the centre. Pour the beaten egg into the well and gradually beat in the milk and water, incorporating the flour as you do so to give a smooth batter.

3. Pour the batter over the vegetables and cook in the oven for 40–45 minutes until puffed up and golden. Serve immediately.

NEW POTATO CASSEROLE WITH FRESH GREENS

Serves 3–4

Dark leafy vegetables have a sorry place in British cookery – the distinctive aroma of overcooked cabbage used to be a feature of all too many school dining rooms. Luckily those days are now history as far as I'm concerned. Spain is the inspiration for this recipe – the Spanish have the knack of taking a few ingredients and making a simple dish of intense flavours that is very satisfying both to cook and to eat. If you ever come across Swiss chard, a vegetable more often found across the Channel, use it here as it will be wonderful.

4 tablespoons olive oil	1 garlic clove, crushed
450 g (1 lb) new potatoes, thinly sliced	1 dried chilli, chopped
1 medium red onion, sliced	3–4 eggs
350 g (12 oz) spring greens or Savoy cabbage, shredded	salt and freshly ground black pepper

1. Preheat the oven to 200°C (400°F, Gas Mark 6). Heat 3 tablespoons of the oil in a large frying pan until very hot, then add the potatoes and onion a few slices at a time to prevent them sticking together, seasoning each layer well. Cook over a medium heat for about 10 minutes, turning occasionally, until the potatoes are golden and tender.

2. Meanwhile, bring a large pan of water to the boil, add the greens and cook for 2 minutes until just wilted. Drain and pat dry with kitchen paper. Heat the remaining tablespoon of oil in a medium pan, add the garlic and chilli and cook for 1 minute until golden. Add the greens and seasoning and stir over a medium heat for 3–4 minutes until just browned. Take care they don't burn.

3. Mix the greens with the potatoes and transfer to a shallow earthenware casserole. Make three or four slight indentations in the top and break an egg into each one. Bake for 8–10 minutes until the eggs are just set, then serve immediately with plenty of crusty bread.

NON-VEGETARIAN TIP

THIS DISH REALLY STANDS ON ITS OWN AS A COMPLETE SUPPER BUT WITHOUT THE EGGS IT COULD BE AN ACCOMPANIMENT TO A MEATY FISH SUCH AS MONKFISH, COD OR HALIBUT. CHOOSE GOOD-SIZED FISH STEAKS, BRUSH WITH OLIVE OIL AND GRILL OR FRY UNTIL TENDER.

NEW POTATO CASSEROLE WITH FRESH GREENS.

Roasted Vegetable Terrine

Serves 6

This recipe was inspired by a wonderful vegetable terrine created by vegetarian caterer Nadine Abensur for BBC Vegetarian Good Food *magazine. It's ideal for parties as it should be made a day in advance to let the flavours develop. Salting aubergines before cooking used to be recommended, as the flesh could be very bitter, but with new varieties it is no longer necessary. I do find that salting stops the aubergines absorbing so much oil when fried, but it's up to you whether you bother or not.*

5 tablespoons olive oil	175 g (6 oz) mascarpone cheese
2 medium aubergines, thinly sliced into rounds	1 garlic clove, crushed
2 yellow peppers	1 tablespoon black olive paste or sun-dried
1 red pepper	tomato paste
3 medium courgettes,	3 tablespoons chopped fresh basil
thinly sliced lengthways	400 g (14 oz) can artichoke hearts, drained
8 baby leeks	salt and freshly ground black pepper

1. Preheat the oven to 220°C (425°F, Gas Mark 7). Heat 4 tablespoons of the olive oil in a pan and fry the aubergine slices in batches until golden on both sides. Drain thoroughly on kitchen paper. Place the peppers on a baking sheet and roast for 10–15 minutes until the skins are blackened. Place them in a plastic bag and leave for 5 minutes for the skins to loosen. Peel off the skins, deseed the peppers and slice into thin strips.

2. Arrange the courgettes on a baking sheet with the whole leeks, brush with the remaining olive oil and season with salt and pepper. Roast in the oven for 15–20 minutes until golden.

3. Place the mascarpone in a bowl and add the garlic, olive or tomato paste and basil. Season well and beat until thoroughly combined.

4. Brush a 23 x 13 cm (9 x 5 in) loaf tin with olive oil and line the base and sides with the aubergine slices. Arrange separate layers of peppers, courgettes, leeks and artichokes in the tin, seasoning each layer and pressing down well, then add a layer of the mascarpone mixture. Layer the remaining vegetables and mascarpone in the same way, then cover with a final layer of aubergine slices. Cover the tin with plastic film and weight down with cans or weights. Chill overnight.

5. To serve the terrine, turn it out on to a large serving plate and cut in thick slices with a sharp serrated knife or an electric carving knife.

Savoy Cabbage and Caraway Cake

Serves 4–6

This savoury cake has a cheesy polenta topping but you can substitute sliced cooked potatoes and a scattering of grated cheese if you like. Serve with a green vegetable such as broccoli and Roasted Root Vegetables (see page 85).

1 medium Savoy cabbage	*FOR THE POLENTA TOPPING*
50 g (2 oz) butter	*175 g (6 oz) instant polenta*
1 teaspoon caraway seeds	*15 g (½ oz) butter*
1 large onion, sliced	*25 g (1 oz) Parmesan, freshly grated*
4 tablespoons double cream	
salt and freshly ground black pepper	
freshly grated Parmesan to finish	

1. Remove six good leaves from the cabbage and blanch them in boiling water for 2 minutes. Remove from the water with a slotted spoon, refresh under cold water, then pat dry with kitchen paper. Cut out the hard central stem of each leaf and use the leaves to line an oiled 20 cm (8 in) loose-bottomed cake tin.

2. Finely shred the remaining cabbage and blanch in the boiling water for 2 minutes. Drain well. Heat half the butter in a frying pan and cook the cabbage for 3 minutes until tender. Stir in the caraway seeds and seasoning, then transfer the mixture to a dish and set aside. Heat the remaining butter in the pan and cook the onion over a low heat for about 10 minutes until golden. Season to taste.

3. For the polenta, put 750 ml (1¼ pints) cold water in a large pan and bring to the boil. Add ½ teaspoon salt and pour in the polenta, stirring continuously. Simmer over a low heat for 5–8 minutes, stirring all the time, until the polenta is thick and coming away from the sides of the pan. Stir in the butter and cheese. Pour into a buttered roasting tin and spread to a thickness of 2.5 cm (1 in). Leave to set, then cut into small triangles.

4. Preheat the oven to 200°C (400°F, Gas Mark 6). To assemble the cake, spoon the cooked cabbage into the lined tin and top with the onion. Arrange the polenta triangles on top and pour over the cream. Sprinkle with Parmesan and bake for 15–20 minutes until the topping is crisp and golden. Serve with Onion Gravy (see page 184).

Non-vegetarian Tip

SERVE AS AN ACCOMPANIMENT TO ROASTED GAMMON OR ANY PORK JOINT.

A Vegetable Barbecue

Serves 4

Traditional barbecues seem to offer little for vegetarians other than the odd piece of corn on the cob, but since I discovered, with the help of Marcella Hazan's wonderful Classic Italian Cook Book, *how well suited vegetables are to the barbecue, my al fresco parties have been transformed (see pages 122-23). I find that meat eaters will happily forego their charred burgers and blackened sausages when offered the wonderful flavours and textures provided by these Mediterranean flame-grilled vegetables. I cook them in stages, as some of the vegetable combinations are better at room temperature, and always use the best extra virgin olive oil. It's also a good idea to have all the ingredients ready chopped and prepared so that you can assemble the components as you go. You can, of course, cook everything under the grill instead of on a barbecue, although the flavours won't be quite the same.*

2 plum tomatoes, halved	*1 tablespoon balsamic vinegar*
1 red pepper, halved	*1 teaspoon chopped fresh rosemary*
2 medium red onions, cut in half across the middle	*1 medium aubergine, cut in half lengthways*
4–6 tablespoons extra virgin olive oil	*4 large flat mushrooms*
2 tablespoons shredded fresh basil	*1 garlic clove, chopped*
50 g (2 oz) smoked mozzarella cheese, sliced	*2 tablespoons chopped fresh flat-leaf parsley*
½ green chilli, seeded and chopped	*salt and freshly ground black pepper*
2 medium courgettes, cut in half lengthways	

1. Light the barbecue. When the coals are ready, place the tomatoes, pepper and onions on the rack cut-side down and cook until they are just charred. Turn carefully, brush the cooked sides with a little olive oil and season lightly, then cook the undersides until lightly charred.

2. Slice the cooked vegetables into wedges and place the tomatoes in a bowl with the basil, mozzarella and 1 tablespoon of the oil. Season and toss gently together, then set aside. Mix the red pepper and onions in a bowl, add 1 tablespoon oil and the chopped chilli, then adjust the seasoning. Set aside.

3. Place the courgettes on the barbecue, brush with a little olive oil, season, and then cook on both sides until golden. Cut into strips and mix with 1 tablespoon of the oil, the balsamic vinegar and rosemary. Adjust the seasoning and set aside.

4. Finally, slash the cut sides of the aubergine with a knife in a criss-cross pattern and place on the rack cut-side down. Remove the stalks from the mushrooms and place, stalk-side down, on the barbecue. Cook for about 3–5 minutes until golden, then turn and brush the cooked sides with olive oil. Scatter with the chopped garlic and parsley and cook until the vegetables are golden underneath and the flesh is tender. Cut the aubergine halves in half again. Serve all the vegetables with lots of garlic bread and a green salad.

AUBERGINE AND POTATO CASSEROLE

Serves 4

This is a hearty dish to serve on a cold winter's night with crusty olive bread to mop up any juices.

3 tablespoons olive oil	1 tablespoon dried oregano
1 large or 2 medium aubergines, sliced	1–2 garlic cloves, finely chopped
1 large onion, sliced	1 dried chilli, finely chopped
450 g (1 lb) potatoes, thinly sliced	3 tablespoons freshly grated Parmesan (optional)
400 g (14 oz) can chopped tomatoes	salt and freshly ground black pepper

1. Preheat the oven to 190°C (375°F, Gas Mark 5). Heat the oil in a frying pan and fry the aubergine slices a few at a time on both sides until golden. Drain thoroughly on kitchen paper.

2. Layer the aubergine, onion, potatoes and tomatoes in a 1.7 litre (3 pint) oven-proof casserole dish, seasoning each layer and scattering them with oregano, garlic and chilli. Finish with a layer of aubergine, then sprinkle over the Parmesan, if using.

3. Bake for 1 hour until the vegetables are tender, covering the top with foil if it gets too brown. Serve with plenty of bread and a green salad.

Emmental and Broccoli Soufflé Potatoes

Serves 4

Baked potatoes filled with a fluffy soufflé mix make a tasty supper dish. You can vary the flavourings for the filling as you wish – I particularly like sun-dried tomatoes with oregano and Pecorino cheese.

4 large baking potatoes, about 225 g (8 oz) each	5 tablespoons semi-skimmed milk
freshly ground sea salt	pinch of cayenne pepper
	50 g (2 oz) Emmental cheese, grated
FOR THE FILLING	1 large egg, separated
75 g (3 oz) broccoli, cut into small florets	1 tablespoon freshly grated Parmesan
15 g (½ oz) butter	salt and freshly ground black pepper
15 g (½ oz) plain flour	

1. Preheat the oven to 200°C (400°F, Gas Mark 6). Scrub the potatoes, prick them all over with a fork and rub with sea salt. Bake for 1 hour until the skins are crisp and the potatoes are tender.

2. Meanwhile, bring a small pan of water to the boil, add the broccoli and cook for 5–8 minutes until tender. Drain thoroughly, then purée in a blender until smooth.

3. Melt the butter in a small pan, stir in the flour and cook for 1 minute. Gradually stir in the milk and bring to the boil, stirring continuously, to give a thick sauce. Stir in the broccoli, cayenne, Emmental and seasoning, then beat in the egg yolk.

4. Cut each potato in half and scoop out the flesh, leaving a thick enough shell for the potato to keep its shape. Mash the flesh and stir it into the broccoli and cheese mixture.

5. Whisk the egg white until stiff, then fold it lightly into the broccoli mixture with a metal spoon. Spoon the filling back into the potato shells, sprinkle with Parmesan and place on a baking sheet. Bake for 12–15 minutes until well risen and golden. Serve immediately.

Lentils and Pulses

Low in fat, high in protein and a valuable source of vitamins, minerals and fibre, lentils and pulses have been cultivated for food since at least 7000 BC. They have always played an important role in peasant dishes, often appearing in combination with other complex starches such as rice or pasta. This is invaluable for vegetarians as such mixtures give the complete combination of amino acids needed to make high-class protein. Pulses are quite bland on their own, but cooked with strong flavours such as spices and herbs they develop a wonderfully subtle, rich flavour which is particularly good for satisfying those who miss the taste of meat. And they make great comfort food.

When entertaining guests I try to think ahead if using pulses, as I prefer the flavour and texture of dried ones that need soaking overnight before use. Cans are a more than adequate substitute if I'm in a hurry and I keep a wide range in stock for emergencies.

Puy Lentils with Wine and Porcini Mushrooms

Serves 4

*Many non-vegetarians think hearty stews that warm you up in the midst of winter
are impossible to find on a meat-free diet. I came up with this dish to prove them wrong.
Dried mushrooms have a depth of flavour that more than compensates for a lack of meat;
paired with Puy lentils they make a meal guaranteed to satisfy the most relentless
carnivore. Puy lentils from France have recently become quite widely available
and are much prized for their earthy yet delicate flavour. Serve this dish on
a bed of celeriac puréed with garlic for the ultimate comfort food.*

15 g (½ oz) dried porcini mushrooms	*175 g (6 oz) Puy lentils*
2 tablespoons olive oil	*1 bay leaf*
1 medium onion, chopped	*few sprigs of fresh thyme*
1 celery stick, chopped	*3 tablespoons chopped fresh parsley*
1 garlic clove, crushed	*1 tablespoon tomato purée*
1 medium carrot, diced	*150 ml (¼ pint) red wine*
350 g (12 oz) mixed mushrooms, such as chestnut,	*300 ml (½ pint) vegetable stock*
oyster, shiitake and field mushrooms,	*(see page 186)*
sliced if large	*salt and freshly ground black pepper*

1. Place the porcini in a bowl, pour over 150 ml (¼ pint) boiling water and leave to
stand for 15 minutes.

2. Heat the olive oil in a medium pan, add the onion, celery, garlic and carrot and
cook, stirring, for 5 minutes until softened but not browned. Drain the soaked
mushrooms, reserving the liquid, and chop finely. Add the dried and fresh mushrooms to the pan and cook for 5 minutes.

3. Add the lentils, bay leaf, thyme, parsley, tomato purée, red wine, vegetable stock,
mushroom liquid and seasoning to the pan. Bring to the boil, cover and simmer for
35–40 minutes until the lentils are tender and the liquid reduced. Check the seasoning and serve with celeriac purée or mashed potatoes.

Non-vegetarian Tip

ADD 225 G (8 OZ) THICKLY SLICED CHORIZO OR OTHER SPICED SAUSAGE TO THE PAN WITH THE
MUSHROOMS, AND COOK AS DIRECTED.

PEPPER AND BEAN HOTPOT

Serves 4

If you wish to use dried beans, soak 275 g (10 oz) dried cannellini beans in cold water overnight and then cook them in fresh water for 1–1½ hours until tender.

1 red pepper	*2 tablespoons tomato purée*
1 yellow pepper	*few drops of Tabasco*
2 tablespoons olive oil	*2 x 425 g (15 oz) cans cannellini beans, drained*
1 large onion, sliced	*salt and freshly ground black pepper*
1 garlic clove, crushed	*chopped fresh parsley to garnish*
400 g (14 oz) can chopped tomatoes	

1. Grill the peppers on all sides under a high heat until blackened. Place in a bag for 5 minutes for the skins to loosen, then peel off the skins and seed and chop the peppers.

2. Heat the oil in a flameproof casserole, add the onion and garlic and cook over a medium heat for 3 minutes until softened. Stir in the tomatoes, tomato purée, Tabasco and seasoning and simmer gently for 15 minutes to give a thick sauce.

3. Add the drained beans and the grilled peppers to the tomato sauce and simmer for 10–15 minutes, stirring occasionally. Check the seasoning and then serve with baked potatoes and salad.

CHICK PEA AND LENTIL CURRY WITH FRESH MINT RAITA

Serves 4

I got the idea for this recipe from Pat Chapman of the Curry Club, who first showed me how well different pulses go together. It's a wonderfully hearty dish that is just as good with baked or mashed potatoes as with basmati rice or naan bread. For a change, I sometimes replace the mint in the raita with fresh coriander.

2 tablespoons sunflower oil	1 tomato, chopped
1 small onion, sliced	425g (15 oz) can chick peas, drained
2 garlic cloves, crushed	
1 teaspoon ground cumin	FOR THE MINT RAITA
2 teaspoons ground coriander	150 ml (¼ pint) yoghurt
½ teaspoon ground turmeric	3 tablespoons chopped fresh mint
¼–½ teaspoon cayenne pepper	pinch of cayenne pepper
1 cinnamon stick	salt
100 g (4 oz) red lentils	

1. Heat the oil in a medium pan and cook the onion and garlic over a medium heat until lightly browned. Add the ground spices and cinnamon stick and cook for a further minute.

2. Add the lentils, tomato and 600 ml (1 pint) cold water to the pan and bring to the boil. Simmer for 20 minutes until the lentils are tender and the liquid has almost evaporated.

3. Meanwhile, make the raita. Mix the yoghurt with the mint, cayenne and a little salt. Set aside.

4. Stir the drained chick peas into the lentils and simmer for 5 minutes to heat through. Check the seasoning and serve with the raita.

CHICK PEA AND TOMATO SALAD

Serves 4

Soaking chick peas can be offputting as it means planning ahead, but it is worth doing as the texture and flavour of dried chick peas are superior to canned. I always try to think ahead and put a bowl on to soak before I go to bed; having said that, though, I would use canned chick peas if in a hurry as they still taste good.

225 g (8 oz) dried chick peas	4 tablespoons extra virgin olive oil
2 garlic cloves, crushed	1 tablespoon red wine vinegar
1 red onion, sliced	3 ripe tomatoes, deseeded and chopped
1 dried chilli, chopped	3 tablespoons chopped fresh basil
1 bay leaf	salt and freshly ground black pepper

1. Cover the chick peas with cold water and leave to soak overnight. The next day, drain the chick peas, place in a pan, then cover with fresh water and bring to the boil. Boil for 10 minutes, then reduce the heat and simmer for $1^1/_2$–2 hours until tender.

2. Drain the chick peas and place them in a bowl with the garlic, onion, chilli, bay leaf, oil and vinegar. Season well and mix thoroughly. Leave to cool.

3. Just before serving, stir the tomatoes and basil into the salad. Serve at room temperature, accompanied by olive bread.

GOLDEN VEGETABLE AND BEAN STEW

Serves 4–6

This thick, warming stew is just the thing to serve on a crisp autumn day, when pumpkins are beginning to appear in the shops. A medium pumpkin should give the correct amount of flesh and will be sweeter and more tender than some of the monsters on sale.

2 tablespoons olive oil	*150 ml (¼ pint) tomato passata*
1 large onion, sliced	*600 ml (1 pint) vegetable stock (see page 186)*
1 leek, sliced	*pinch of saffron strands*
2 garlic cloves, chopped	*425 g (15 oz) can borlotti beans, drained*
2 celery sticks, sliced	*salt and freshly ground black pepper*
1 medium carrot, sliced	*chopped fresh basil to garnish*
225 g (8 oz) swede, cut into 2.5 cm (1 in) chunks	*freshly grated Parmesan and extra virgin*
175 g (6 oz) potato, cut into 2.5 cm (1 in) chunks	*olive oil to serve*
350 g (12 oz) pumpkin flesh, cut into 2.5 cm (1 in) chunks	

1. Heat the olive oil in a large flameproof casserole. Add the onion, leek and garlic and cook for 5 minutes until softened. Add the remaining vegetables and cook for 8–10 minutes until they are just turning golden.

2. Pour in the tomato passata and stock with the saffron strands and plenty of seasoning. Bring to the boil and simmer for 20–25 minutes until the vegetables are tender. Stir in the borlotti beans and simmer for a couple of minutes longer. Garnish with fresh basil and serve with freshly grated Parmesan and a drizzle of extra virgin olive oil.

NON-VEGETARIAN TIP

FRY 225 G (8 OZ) GAMMON STEAK, CUT INTO STRIPS, WITH THE ONION, LEEK AND GARLIC AND CONTINUE AS ABOVE.

GOLDEN VEGETABLE AND BEAN STEW.

Vegetable Cassoulet

Serves 6–8

The flavours of this hearty bean stew improve with keeping, so make it the day before you need it and reheat. You can also freeze it minus the breadcrumb topping.

350 g (12 oz) dried haricot beans	*1 green pepper, seeded and chopped*
3 medium onions	*90 ml (3 fl oz) dry white wine*
4 cloves	*2 x 400 g (14 oz) cans chopped tomatoes*
1 carrot	*1 tablespoon tomato purée*
1 bouquet garni	*2 teaspoons paprika*
1 bay leaf	*2 large aubergines, sliced*
4 tablespoons olive oil	*50 g (2 oz) fresh white breadcrumbs*
2 garlic cloves, chopped	*salt and freshly ground black pepper*
2 red peppers, seeded and chopped	

1. Cover the beans with cold water and leave to soak overnight. The next day, drain the beans and place them in a large pan. Peel and halve one of the onions and stud it with the cloves, then add it to the pan with the carrot, bouquet garni and bay leaf. Add enough cold water to cover and bring to the boil. Cover and simmer for 1–1½ hours until the beans are just tender. Season halfway through the cooking time. Drain the beans, reserving the cooking liquid. Discard the carrot, onion, bay leaf and bouquet garni.

2. Chop the remaining onions and cook them in half the oil for 5 minutes until golden. Add the garlic and peppers and cook for 10 minutes until soft and golden. Stir in the wine, tomatoes, tomato purée, paprika and seasoning, bring to the boil and simmer for 5 minutes.

3. Preheat the oven to 170°C (325°F, Gas Mark 3). Heat the remaining oil in a frying pan and fry the aubergine on both sides until golden. Drain on kitchen paper.

4. Layer the haricot beans, tomato mixture and aubergines in a large ovenproof casserole, finishing with a layer of beans. Pour over enough of the bean cooking liquid just to reach the top of the beans. Cover and bake for 1 hour.

5. Remove the casserole from the oven, uncover and sprinkle over the breadcrumbs, spooning up the liquid to soak them thoroughly. Increase the oven temperature to 200°C (400°F, Gas Mark 6) and bake the casserole, uncovered, for a further 30 minutes until the topping is golden. Serve with crusty bread and a salad.

Red Bean and Potato Chilli

Serves 4

I make this chilli for family get-togethers as it's popular with all ages. For large gatherings you could make two versions, one hot and one mild, and serve with garlic bread.

3 tablespoons olive oil	1 bay leaf
225 g (8 oz) chestnut mushrooms, quartered	225 g (8 oz) tomato passata
1 large onion, sliced	300 ml (½ pint) vegetable stock (see page 186)
2 garlic cloves, chopped	350 g (12 oz) potatoes, cubed
2 teaspoons paprika	2 x 425 g (15 oz) cans red kidney beans, drained
1 teaspoon ground cumin	salt and freshly ground black pepper
1–2 teaspoons chilli powder	chopped fresh parsley to garnish
1 tablespoon chopped fresh marjoram	

1. Heat 2 tablespoons of the oil in a large pan and fry the mushrooms for 5 minutes until golden. Remove with a slotted spoon and set aside.

2. Add the remaining oil to the pan and fry the onion and garlic for 3 minutes until softened. Stir in the paprika, cumin, chilli, marjoram and seasoning and cook for a further minute. Add the bay leaf, tomato passata, stock and potatoes and bring to the boil. Cover and simmer for 20 minutes until the potatoes are tender.

3. Add the mushrooms to the pan with the kidney beans and simmer, uncovered, for 15 minutes. Check the seasoning and serve garnished with parsley.

Non-vegetarian Tip

SERVE WITH GRILLED SAUSAGES.

Chick Pea, Rocket and Yellow Pepper Tortilla

I make a tortilla for supper most weeks and any leftovers are excellent cut into cubes and served as an appetizer or sliced for picnics and packed lunches.

1 small yellow pepper	50 g (2 oz) cooked chick peas
5 tablespoons olive oil	50 g (2 oz) rocket
1 medium onion, sliced	5 eggs
2 medium potatoes, cooked in their skins and thickly sliced	salt and freshly ground black pepper

1. Grill the pepper under a high heat until blackened on all sides, then place in a plastic bag for 5 minutes for the skin to loosen. Peel off the skin, deseed and cut into strips.

2. Heat half the oil in a frying pan, add the onion and potatoes, seasoning well, and cook for 8–10 minutes until golden. Add the chick peas, pepper strips and rocket and continue cooking for 5 minutes. Drain the vegetables in a sieve.

3. Beat the eggs in a bowl, add the drained vegetables and stir to combine. Leave to stand for 5 minutes.

4. Heat the remaining oil in a 20 cm (8 in) frying pan, add the egg mixture and cook over a low-medium heat for 5–8 minutes until the egg is set on top and golden underneath. Carefully turn the mixture out on to a large plate and then slide it back into the pan for 5 minutes to cook the other side. Turn again twice until the tortilla is cooked in the centre. Serve warm or cold with a tomato and onion salad.

Chick Pea, Rocket and Yellow Pepper Tortilla.

Sweetcorn Chick Pea Fritters with Mint Chutney

Serves 4

Gram flour is made from ground chick peas and is available in Indian stores and some large supermarkets. It has a superb nutty flavour that is ideal for vegetable fritters and savoury pancakes. These fritters can be served as a main course with basmati rice or made smaller for a starter or a nibble with drinks.

	For the mint chutney
100 g (4 oz) gram flour	
½ teaspoon salt	1 green chilli, deseeded and finely chopped
½ teaspoon bicarbonate of soda	1 red onion, finely chopped
350 g (12 oz) can sweetcorn, drained	4 tablespoons chopped fresh mint
½ teaspoon chilli powder	2 tablespoons fresh lime juice
2 tablespoons chopped fresh coriander	salt
1 tablespoon sesame seeds	
2 tablespoons lemon juice	
sunflower oil for frying	

1. First prepare the chutney. Mix all the ingredients together in a small bowl and set aside. For the fritters, sift the flour, salt and bicarbonate of soda into a mixing bowl. Stir in the sweetcorn, chilli, coriander, sesame seeds and lemon juice and add 4–6 tablespoons of water to give a thick batter.

2. Heat 2.5 cm (1 in) sunflower oil in a large frying pan and drop tablespoonfuls of the mixture into the hot oil. Cook for a couple of minutes until golden underneath, then turn and cook the other side. Drain on kitchen paper and serve with the mint chutney.

CANNELLINI BEAN PURÉE WITH ROSEMARY AND GARLIC

Serves 4

This delicately flavoured purée makes a wonderful main course served with Focaccia with Chilli and Tomato (see page 178) and a salad of rocket and shaved Parmesan, or as an accompaniment to dishes such as Asparagus, Red Pepper and Goat's Cheese Slice (see page 70).

225 g (8 oz) dried cannellini beans	1 small head of garlic
2 bay leaves	5 tablespoons extra virgin olive oil
4 large sprigs of fresh rosemary	2 tablespoons lemon juice
1 carrot	salt and freshly ground black pepper
1 small onion	fresh rosemary sprigs to garnish
6 peppercorns	

1. Cover the beans with cold water and leave to soak overnight. The next day, drain the beans and place them in a pan with the bay leaves, half the rosemary, the carrot, onion, peppercorns and water to cover. Bring to the boil and cook for 10 minutes, then reduce the heat and simmer for 1–1½ hours until tender. Drain the beans, discarding the herbs and vegetables. Reserve 150 ml (¼ pint) of the cooking liquid.

2. While the beans are cooking, peel the cloves of garlic and place them in a small heavy-based pan with half the olive oil and the remaining rosemary. Cook over a very low heat for about 15 minutes until the garlic is very soft and golden; keep an eye on it to make sure it doesn't burn. Discard the rosemary.

3. Place the drained beans in a food processor with the lemon juice, seasoning and the cooked garlic and its oil. Blend until smooth, then, with the motor running, gradually drizzle in the remaining oil and enough of the reserved cooking liquid to give a light, smooth purée. Pile into a serving dish, garnish with rosemary sprigs and serve.

NON-VEGETARIAN TIP

SERVE WITH GRILLED LAMB CHOPS OR YOUR FAVOURITE SAUSAGES.

SPICED BEANS WITH SAFFRON RICE

Serves 4

The combination of rice and pulses is a classic one found in cuisines around the world. Nutritionally it works well for vegetarians as it combines the nine essential amino acids that make a complete protein. This dish is great for parties as it can be made in advance and heated through when you need it. If you can't find aduki beans, black-eye beans or red kidney beans also work well. Serve with Mint Raita (see page 104) and chutneys.

175 g (6 oz) aduki beans	½ teaspoon turmeric
350 g (12 oz) basmati rice	1 teaspoon garam masala
¼ teaspoon saffron strands	200 g (7 oz) can chopped tomatoes
25 g (1 oz) butter, diced	salt
2 medium onions	
2 tablespoons sunflower oil	TO FINISH
1 teaspoon cumin seeds	1 small onion, sliced
2 cloves garlic, finely chopped	1 tablespoon sunflower oil
1 cm (½ in) piece fresh root ginger, finely chopped	25 g (1 oz) blanched almonds
1 green chilli, seeded and finely chopped	25 g (1 oz) raisins
2 teaspoons ground coriander	fresh coriander sprigs to garnish

1. Cover the beans with cold water and leave to soak overnight. The next day, drain the beans and place them in a pan with 600 ml (1 pint) water. Bring to the boil and cook for 10 minutes, then cover and simmer for 30 minutes until the water has nearly evaporated and the beans are tender. Set aside.

2. While the beans are cooking, wash the rice in several changes of water, then cover with fresh water and leave to soak for 30 minutes. Pour 2 tablespoons hot water over the saffron. Drain the rice and place it in a pan with the saffron liquid and the butter. Add 600 ml (1 pint) cold water and some salt and bring to the boil. Reduce the heat, cover tightly and simmer for 10 minutes, then remove from the heat and leave to stand, covered, for 5 minutes. Fluff up with a fork.

3. Preheat the oven to 200°C (400°F, Gas Mark 6). Slice one onion thinly and chop the other. Heat the oil in a large frying pan and fry the sliced onion until golden.

SPICED BEANS WITH SAFFRON RICE.

Remove from the pan with a slotted spoon and stir it into the rice. Add the cumin seeds to the pan and cook for 30 seconds, then stir in the chopped onion, with the garlic, ginger and chilli. Cook for 5 minutes until just golden.

4. Stir in the spices and cook for a further minute, then stir in the tomatoes and simmer for 5 minutes until they form a thick sauce. Stir in the cooked aduki beans and season to taste with salt.

5. Spoon a third of the rice into a large deep earthenware dish. Spoon over half the bean mixture, followed by another layer of rice, then the rest of the beans. Finish with the remaining rice. Cover the dish with foil and bake for 20–25 minutes until piping hot.

6. To finish, fry the onion in the oil until golden, add the almonds and raisins and cook for a further minute. Scatter this mixture over the rice and garnish with fresh coriander sprigs.

Salads and Accompaniments

$\mathcal{V}$EGETABLE ACCOMPANIMENTS to vegetarian main dishes may seem like overdoing it when vegetables make up the bulk of the central recipe, and it can be difficult to decide what to serve to complement the main course. If this is the case and you are basing a menu around a recipe such as a vegetable ragout, then I think the key should be simplicity. Always serve a starch such as good bread, rice, potatoes or pasta – rice and bread for runny sauces, soups and stews that need something to mop up the juices; pasta and potatoes with drier, unsauced dishes. Remember, to follow the current recommendations on healthy eating you should ensure that starchy foods make up about 40 per cent of your daily intake – a good way to achieve this is to serve bread with every meal.

When deciding which other vegetables to serve, consider the colours and textures of your main dish and try to choose foods that complement and contrast. You can rarely go wrong if you offer a bowlful of assorted salad leaves with a well-made dressing, and if the main course swamps or overwhelms a salad, then serve it French-style as a course on its own.

FENNEL GRATIN

Serves 4

Until recently I wasn't a great fan of fennel, as in its raw state it tastes all too strongly of aniseed balls for my liking. However, since rediscovering it in its cooked form I have become a convert. Baked with Parmesan, as it is here, the aniseed flavour is softened into a subtle presence that makes an ideal partner for the cheese. Serve this dish as an accompaniment or starter.

4 medium fennel bulbs, about 100 g (4 oz) each, cut into quarters	*50 g (2 oz) Parmesan, freshly grated*
	25 g (1 oz) butter
2 tablespoons extra virgin olive oil	*salt and freshly ground black pepper*

1. Preheat the oven to 200°C (400°F, Gas Mark 6). Bring a large pan of water to the boil, add the fennel and simmer for about 5 minutes until almost tender. Drain thoroughly, toss with the olive oil and seasoning and arrange in an oiled roasting tin or gratin dish.

2. Sprinkle the Parmesan cheese over the fennel and dot with the butter. Bake for 20 minutes until the cheese is melted and golden.

SPICED MANGO AND AVOCADO SALAD

Serves 4

This salad doubles up as a refreshing starter on a hot day.

1 ripe mango	*FOR THE DRESSING*
2 ripe avocados	*1 tablespoon lime juice*
juice of ½ lime	*2 tablespoons sunflower oil*
fresh coriander sprigs and lime wedges to garnish	*2 spring onions, shredded*
	½ teaspoon mild curry paste
	salt and freshly ground black pepper

1. Cut the mango and avocados away from their stones, then peel carefully and cut the flesh into strips 5 cm (2 in) long. Arrange in a serving dish and sprinkle with the lime juice.

2. Put all the dressing ingredients in a screw-topped jar and shake until blended. Pour the dressing over the mango and avocado and toss gently to coat. Garnish with coriander sprigs and lime wedges and serve.

MARINATED MUSHROOM SALAD WITH SESAME DRESSING

Serves 4

350 g (12 oz) chestnut mushrooms, sliced	*FOR THE DRESSING*
3 celery sticks, chopped	*4 tablespoons sunflower oil*
1 small red onion, sliced	*2 tablespoons red wine vinegar*
½ red chilli, seeded and chopped	*1 tablespoon sesame oil*
2 tablespoons chopped fresh coriander	*1 tablespoon dark muscovado sugar*
1 teaspoon toasted sesame seeds	*1 garlic clove, crushed*
	salt and freshly ground black pepper

1. Place the mushrooms, celery, onion and chilli in a bowl and stir well.

2. Put all the dressing ingredients in a bowl and whisk until combined. Pour the dressing over the mushrooms, cover and leave to stand for at least 2 hours, stirring occasionally.

3. Just before serving, stir the coriander and toasted sesame seeds into the salad and transfer to a serving dish.

French Beans with Roasted Almonds

Serves 4

This can be served warm as a vegetable accompaniment (see page 71).

450 g (1 lb) French beans, topped and tailed	FOR THE DRESSING
2 tablespoons olive oil	3 tablespoons extra virgin olive oil
50 g (2 oz) blanched almonds	1 tablespoon lemon juice
coarse sea salt	2 tablespoons chopped fresh flat-leaf parsley
	salt and freshly ground black pepper

1. Cook the beans in boiling water for 3 minutes until almost tender. Drain and refresh under cold water, then drain again and pat dry with kitchen paper. Place in a salad bowl.

2. Whisk together all the dressing ingredients until combined. Pour the dressing over the beans, toss gently to coat and leave to cool.

3. Just before serving, heat the olive oil in a frying pan and fry the almonds until just golden. Drain on kitchen paper and sprinkle with coarse salt. Scatter the almonds over the salad and serve.

Warm Courgette Salad

Serves 4

I have grown a single courgette plant in a growbag on my patio for the last couple of years. The resulting courgettes are small, tender and have a marvellous flavour that needs little enhancing. I use them in this salad or in stir fries.

450 g (1 lb) small courgettes	3 tablespoons chopped fresh herbs, such as chives,
3–4 tablespoons extra virgin olive oil	parsley, tarragon and basil
2 garlic cloves, thinly sliced	salt and freshly ground black pepper
1 tablespoon balsamic vinegar	

1. Cut the courgettes into thick matchsticks about 5 cm (2 in) long. Heat the oil in a frying pan, add the courgettes and toss them over a high heat for about 2 minutes until almost tender and beginning to brown. Remove with a slotted spoon and place in a salad bowl.

2. Add the garlic to the pan and cook for 30 seconds. Stir in the vinegar, herbs and seasoning and pour over the courgettes. Toss gently and serve.

New Potato Salad with Tarragon and Orange

Serves 4

I adore Jersey Royal potatoes and, during their short season in May and June, eat them for as many meals as possible. The tiny Jerseys need only a little butter and chives to enhance their wonderful flavour and texture. This salad can also be made with the larger potatoes that come into the shops at the end of June or the pink fir apple potatoes now available in many supermarkets.

680 g (1½ lb) new potatoes, preferably Jersey Royals, scrubbed	FOR THE DRESSING
	1 tablespoon red wine vinegar
2 oranges	3 tablespoons olive oil
1 bunch spring onions, chopped	1 tablespoon chopped fresh tarragon
	salt and freshly ground black pepper

1. Halve any larger potatoes and cook them in boiling water for 10–15 minutes until just tender. Drain and place in a salad bowl. Whisk together the dressing ingredients and pour them over the hot potatoes. Toss gently to coat, then leave to cool to room temperature.

2. Just before serving, carefully peel the oranges with a serrated knife removing all the white pith. Cut them into thin slices and then cut each slice into quarters. Add to the potatoes with the spring onions and toss gently.

Overleaf: A Vegetable Barbecue (see page 98) served with New Potato Salad with Tarragon and Orange, Fresh Beetroot Salad with Caraway (see page 127) and Red Onion and Pine Nut Focaccia Rolls (see page 181).

Honey- and Mustard-roasted New Potatoes and Shallots

Serves 4

If you can get the larger, elongated shallots they work well here.

4 tablespoons olive oil	1 tablespoon clear honey
450 g (1 lb) even-sized new potatoes	1 teaspoon coarse-grained mustard
225 g (8 oz) shallots, peeled (see page 37)	coarse sea salt and freshly ground
4 sprigs of fresh thyme	black pepper

1. Preheat the oven to 200°C (400°F, Gas Mark 6). Put the oil in a small roasting tin and heat through in the oven for a couple of minutes. Add the potatoes and shallots to the pan and toss until coated in the hot oil. Add the thyme and seasoning.

2. Roast for about 30 minutes, then drizzle with the honey and stir in the mustard. Mix well to coat the vegetables and return to the oven for a further 15 minutes until golden. Serve immediately.

Lemon-glazed Carrots with Poppy Seeds

Serves 4

If you don't like the crunch of poppy seeds, use toasted sesame seeds or pine nuts instead.

450 g (1 lb) carrots, cut into thin matchsticks	1 teaspoon poppy seeds
25 g (1 oz) butter	2 tablespoons chopped fresh flat-leaf parsley
1 teaspoon caster sugar	salt and freshly ground black pepper
grated rind and juice of ½ lemon	

1. Place the carrots in a heavy-based pan with the butter, sugar, lemon rind and juice and 150 ml (¼ pint) water. Bring to the boil and simmer gently for 10 minutes until the carrots are tender and lightly glazed and the liquid has evaporated.

2. Stir the poppy seeds, parsley and seasoning into the carrots and cook for a minute or two. Serve immediately.

LEAFY SALAD WITH CROUTONS AND PINE NUT DRESSING

Serves 4

This dressing was created by my husband Mark. He is always called on to make salad dressings for the family as he seems to have the knack of balancing the acid and oil, which I can never match even when following the same recipe. The dressing also works well on any bitter salad leaves, such as frisée or watercress, or on roasted vegetable salads.

100 g (4 oz) rocket	FOR THE PINE NUT DRESSING
100 g (4 oz) lamb's lettuce	25 g (1 oz) pine nuts
50 g (2 oz) cherry tomatoes, halved	2 garlic cloves, peeled
1 thick slice country-style bread	4 tablespoons freshly grated Parmesan
2 tablespoons olive oil	1 tablespoon balsamic vinegar
	4 tablespoons extra virgin olive oil
	salt and freshly ground black pepper

1. To make the dressing, place the pine nuts and garlic in a pestle and mortar and crush to a smooth paste. Using the pestle, gradually work in the cheese and vinegar, then drizzle in the oil a little at a time, keeping the dressing thick. Season to taste.

2. Wash and dry the salad leaves and place them in a salad bowl with the cherry tomatoes. Remove the crusts from the bread and cut it into cubes.

3. Heat the oil in a small frying pan and fry the bread cubes over a medium heat until golden. Drain on kitchen paper. Add the croutons to the salad, then pour over the dressing and toss gently to coat. Serve immediately.

Spinach with Raisins and Pine Nuts

Serves 4

This recipe comes from the Catalan region of Spain and the presence of the pine nuts and raisins shows the Moorish influence on that country's cuisine. Spring greens are also excellent prepared this way (see pages 166-67).

450 g (1 lb) fresh spinach	25 g (1 oz) pine nuts
2 tablespoons olive oil	25 g (1 oz) raisins
1 small red onion, sliced	salt and freshly ground black pepper
1 garlic clove, chopped	

1. Wash the spinach and place it in a pan with only the water clinging to its leaves. Cover the pan and cook gently for 3–4 minutes until tender. Drain thoroughly, squeezing to remove any excess water, then chop roughly.

2. Heat the oil in a frying pan, add the onion and garlic and cook for 3 minutes until softened. Add the pine nuts and raisins and cook for a minute or two until the pine nuts are golden. Add the spinach and stir until heated through. Season well and serve immediately.

Fresh Beetroot Salad with Caraway

Serves 4

It is now quite common to find fresh raw beetroot in the vegetable section of many supermarkets, and if you've only ever tasted the vinegary cooked root, preparing it yourself will be a revelation. It has a wonderful sweet, subtle flavour and is as good served hot (see Roasted Beetroot with Soured Cream and Horseradish on page 26) as in a salad. If you take care not to damage the skin, the beetroot will not bleed purple juice everywhere but it does need a good scrub to remove any dirt before cooking. This is a very simple salad but it's one of my favourites and can also be made with bought pre-cooked beetroot as long as it has been prepared without vinegar (see pages 122-23).

450 g (1 lb) fresh beetroot, scrubbed	FOR THE DRESSING
3 tablespoons chopped fresh flat-leaf parsley	3 tablespoons extra virgin olive oil
	2 teaspoons lemon juice
	1 tablespoon caraway seeds
	salt and freshly ground black pepper

1. Put the beetroot in a pan of cold water, bring to the boil and simmer, covered, for 1–1¼ hours until tender (to speed things up you can cook the beetroot in the microwave – I find 225 g (8 oz) beetroot takes about 12–15 minutes in a 750 watt oven on High). Drain, leave to cool for 5 minutes and then peel off the skin.

2. Cut the beetroot into 5 cm (2 in) matchsticks and place in a serving dish. Whisk together all the dressing ingredients and pour them over the beetroot. Toss gently and leave to cool. Just before serving, scatter over the chopped parsley.

Roast Baby Artichoke and Aubergine Salad

On the whole I have been disappointed by the baby vegetables now available in supermarkets as I find them lacking in flavour. Baby aubergines and artichokes are the exception but this may be because they look so attractive when cooked and, in the case of the artichokes, they are much easier to cook and eat than larger ones. They work well in this salad, which makes a great accompaniment to a tortilla such as the one on page 110.

225 g (8 oz) baby aubergines	1 tablespoon lemon juice
225 g (8 oz) baby artichokes	1 garlic clove, crushed
1 medium red onion	1 teaspoon capers, chopped
	2 tablespoons chopped fresh parsley
FOR THE DRESSING	salt and freshly ground black pepper
4 tablespoons extra virgin olive oil	

1. Preheat the oven to 180°C (350°F, Gas Mark 4). Cut the aubergines, artichokes and onion in half lengthways then in half again. Place on a baking sheet and cook for 30 minutes, turning occasionally, until golden and just tender. Place in a serving dish.

2. Whisk together all the dressing ingredients and pour them over the vegetables. Let the vegetables cool to room temperature, then serve.

Hot Puddings

I HAVE INHERITED my sweet tooth and love of puddings from my father, a real traditionalist when it comes to all things culinary. As a child, I loved all the wonderful puddings that his mother, my grandmother, prepared for us – creamy rice pudding with a sprinkling of nutmeg, steamed jam 'top-hat' pudding and, best of all, semolina with a spoonful of jam stirred through it.

I now enjoy making such puds for my own children, and they show the same enthusiasm for them that I did. During the winter, Sunday lunch in our house is a social occasion, an opportunity to sit down with friends and their families, and of course the food plays a vital part. Everyone enjoys an old fashioned-pudding such as Lemon Bread and Butter Pudding (page 132) or Carrot and Marmalade Pudding (page 130). And I'm never allowed to forget the custard! (Make it in the microwave for speed and convenience.) I also find that such old-fashioned puddings go down well at supper parties and even on more formal occasions, but do make sure your pudding doesn't follow a heavy main course or your guests' digestion may suffer. Of course, hot puddings are not necessarily heavyweights by definition. Fruit dishes can add a welcome sharpness at the end of a meal.

Hot puddings have the added advantage that they are usually very simple and quick to prepare. I often serve Red Fruit Compote (page 138) or Apricot Toffee Pudding (page 136) when entertaining mid-week as they can be whipped up in minutes, put on to steam or bake and then left to their own devices while I get on with preparing the rest of the meal.

CARROT AND MARMALADE PUDDING

Serves 6

Carrots are a natural sweetener and give a wonderfully moist texture to puddings and cakes. This pudding is made with breadcrumbs instead of flour. You can use brown or white bread but make sure the loaf is at least a day old or the pudding will be heavy.

175 g (6 oz) carrots, coarsely grated	½ teaspoon mixed spice
50 g (2 oz) raisins, preferably Lexia	1 teaspoon ground ginger
175 g (6 oz) fresh breadcrumbs	grated rind of 1 lemon
75 g (3 oz) light muscovado sugar	2 eggs
100 g (4 oz) vegetarian suet	3 tablespoons semi-skimmed milk
½ teaspoon baking powder	4 tablespoons marmalade

1. Place the carrots, raisins, breadcrumbs and sugar in a mixing bowl and stir in the suet, baking powder, spices and lemon rind.

2. Beat the eggs with the milk and stir into the dry ingredients to give a soft dropping consistency. Spoon the marmalade into the base of a buttered 1.2 litre (2 pint) pudding basin, then spoon in the pudding mixture.

3. Cover the pudding securely with greaseproof paper and foil, pleated in the centre, and tie with string. Steam the pudding for 2 hours, topping up the pan with boiling water to prevent it boiling dry. Turn the pudding out on to a warmed serving dish and serve with custard or pouring cream.

Lemon Bread and Butter Pudding

Serves 4

Bread and butter pudding has enjoyed renewed popularity with the revival of traditional British cookery. This version uses cinnamon raisin bread but you could use an enriched bread such as brioche and add raisins and spice.

8 thick slices cinnamon raisin bread	2 tablespoons whisky
25 g (1 oz) butter	200 ml (7 fl oz) milk
3 tablespoons good-quality lemon curd	200 ml (7 fl oz) double cream
3 eggs	caster sugar for sprinkling
25 g (1 oz) golden caster sugar	

1. Preheat the oven to 170°C (325F, Gas Mark 3). Butter the bread and make it into sandwiches with the lemon curd. Cut into triangles and arrange in a 1.2 litre (2 pint) ovenproof dish.

2. Whisk the eggs with the sugar and whisky until pale and frothy. Heat the milk and cream together until almost boiling, then pour on to the eggs, whisking as you do so. Pour this mixture over the bread.

3. Place the dish in a roasting tin half-filled with hot water and bake for 45 minutes until the top is puffy and golden. Sprinkle with caster sugar, place briefly under a hot grill to glaze the top and serve.

Sugar-glazed Sweet Potato Gratin

Serves 4–6

This is a sweet version of Dauphinoise potatoes, made with sweet potatoes, spices and cream. It's a popular pud for Sunday lunch and always generates interest.

100 g (4 oz) dark muscovado sugar	50 g (2 oz) butter, diced
1½ teaspoons ground cardamom	grated rind of 1 lemon
½ teaspoon freshly grated nutmeg	150 ml (¼ pint) double cream
680 g (1½ lb) sweet potatoes, thinly sliced	150 ml (¼ pint) milk
75 g (3 oz) raisins	2 tablespoons rum (optional)

1. Preheat the oven to 180°C (350°F, Gas Mark 4). Mix the sugar with the spices. Layer the sweet potatoes in a buttered 25 x 20 cm (10 x 8 in) baking dish, sprinkling each layer with the sugar and raisins and dotting with the butter. Finish with a layer of potato and dot with any remaining butter and sugar.

2. Place the lemon rind, cream, milk and rum, if using, in a small pan and heat until almost boiling. Pour this mixture over the potatoes and bake for 40 minutes or until the potatoes are tender and the liquid has been absorbed. Serve immediately with clotted cream.

APRICOT AND GINGER CRUMBLE

Serves 4

I love crumbles; they're quick to make, full of wonderful fruity flavours and great hot or cold. I often serve one at more formal dinner parties – fresh raspberry crumble, accompanied by kirsch-flavoured cream, always goes down well. This recipe is my family version but you could dress it up for a dinner party by using poached fresh apricots and adding 15 g (½ oz) ground walnuts to the topping. Fresh ginger is not usually associated with sweet dishes but works very well. It's a lot more subtle than ground ginger and doesn't swamp the flavour of the fruit.

2 x 425 g (15 oz) cans apricot halves in natural juice	*FOR THE CRUMBLE TOPPING*
	175 g (6 oz) wholemeal flour
2.5 cm (1 in) piece fresh root ginger, grated	*½ teaspoon baking powder*
	50 g (2 oz) butter, diced
	75 g (3 oz) demerara sugar
	½ teaspoon ground cinnamon

1. Preheat the oven to 180°C (350°F, Gas Mark 4). Drain the fruit, reserving 4 tablespoons juice. Place the apricots, reserved juice and grated ginger in a shallow ovenproof dish.

2. To make the topping, mix the flour and baking powder together in a mixing bowl and rub in the butter until the mixture resembles fine breadcrumbs. Stir in the sugar and cinnamon.

3. Spread the crumble mixture over the fruit and level the surface. Bake for 35–40 minutes until golden on top and then serve immediately with thin cream or custard.

BAKED FIGS WITH ORANGE

Serves 4

This is one of the simplest recipes I know and one of the most delicious. It also works well with fresh peaches and apricots.

8 ripe figs	grated rind and juice of 1 orange
50 g (2 oz) unsalted butter, diced	150 ml (¼ pint) double cream
50 g (2 oz) light muscovado sugar	

1. Preheat the oven to 220°C (425°F, Gas Mark 7). Cut the figs into quarters and arrange in a single layer in a shallow gratin or baking dish.

2. Scatter the butter, sugar and orange rind over the figs and pour over the juice. Bake for 25–30 minutes until tender, then remove the dish from the oven and pour over the cream. Serve warm or at room temperature.

BAKED FIGS WITH ORANGE.

Apricot Toffee Pudding

This is my version of the incredibly popular sticky toffee pudding that appears on so many menus these days. I actually find many of them too sweet and sticky and so this is somewhat lighter than most.

50 g (2 oz) no–need–to–soak dried apricots	¼ teaspoon ground nutmeg
25 g (1 oz) no–need–to–soak prunes	3–4 tablespoons milk
50 g (2 oz) butter	25 g (1 oz) walnut pieces, chopped
75 g (3 oz) light muscovado sugar	
1 size-3 egg, beaten	FOR THE TOPPING
100 g (4 oz) plain flour	75 g (3 oz) dark muscovado sugar
½ teaspoon baking powder	25 g (1 oz) butter
¼ teaspoon ground cinnamon	3 tablespoons double cream

1. First make the topping. Put all the ingredients in a small pan and stir over a low heat until melted. Bring to the boil and simmer for 1 minute, then pour into a buttered 900 ml (1½ pint) pudding basin.

2. Process or finely chop the apricots and prunes. Cream the butter with the sugar until light and fluffy, then beat in the egg. Sift the flour with the baking powder and spices and fold into the creamed mixture with the milk to give a soft dropping consistency. Stir in the walnuts and the dried fruit.

3. Spoon the mixture into the pudding basin and smooth the surface. Cover the basin with greaseproof paper and foil, making a pleat in the centre, and tie securely with string.

4. Steam the pudding for 1½ hours, making sure the pan doesn't boil dry. Turn out and serve with pouring cream.

LEMON AND APPLE STEAMED PUDDING

Serves 6

In the classic Sussex pond pudding butter, brown sugar and a whole lemon are encased in suet pastry and cooked to a tender, melting and totally luscious mass. I've added tart cooking apples and ginger, which produces quite a different pudding but one no less delicious. It needs a long cooking time to ensure the lemon is soft so don't make it unless you can prepare it well ahead and have space on the hob for a pan to simmer away for 3 hours.

350 g (12 oz) self-raising flour	100 g (4 oz) butter, diced
1 teaspoon ground ginger	100 g (4 oz) demerara sugar
175 g (6 oz) vegetarian suet	350 g (12 oz) cooking apples, peeled,
grated rind of 1 lemon	cored and sliced
1 whole lemon	

1. Sift the flour and ginger into a mixing bowl and stir in the suet and lemon rind. Mix to a soft dough with about 300 ml (½ pint) cold water.

2. On a lightly floured surface, roll out the suet pastry to a large circle. Cut out about a quarter of the pastry in a wedge shape and set aside for the lid. Use the remaining pastry to line a buttered 1.5 litre (2½ pint) pudding basin. Prick the lemon all over with a skewer. Mix the butter with the sugar, then layer them in the pudding basin with the apple slices, placing the whole lemon in the centre.

3. Re-roll the remaining pastry to a circle and use to cover the pudding, pinching the edges together to seal. Cover the basin securely with greaseproof paper and foil, pleated in the centre, and tie with string.

4. Steam the pudding for about 3 hours, by which time the pastry should be cooked through and the lemon completely soft. Top up the pan regularly with boiling water to prevent it boiling dry. Turn the pudding out into a deep serving dish and serve immediately with double cream or custard.

Red Fruit Compote with Cardamom Dumplings

Serves 4

Cardamom is one of my favourite spices in both savoury and sweet dishes. Here it adds its distinctive flavour to little dumplings, but if it's not to your taste you could substitute cinnamon. You can vary the fruit for this compote with the seasons and change the spicing to match; for example, ginger and orange rind go very well with rhubarb.

100 g (4 oz) redcurrants	*For the dumplings*
225 g (8 oz) raspberries	*50 g (2 oz) self-raising flour*
225 g (8 oz) strawberries, halved	*large pinch of ground cardamom*
175 g (6 oz) red cherries, stoned	*1 teaspoon grated lemon rind*
75 g (3 oz) caster sugar	*25 g (1 oz) butter*
	2 teaspoons caster sugar
	2–3 tablespoons semi-skimmed milk

1. Wash the fruit and place it in a large shallow pan or a frying pan with the sugar. Heat gently for 5 minutes until the juices run.

2. Meanwhile, make the dumplings. Sift the flour and cardamom into a bowl and stir in the lemon rind. Rub in the butter until the mixture resembles coarse bread-crumbs, then stir in the sugar and mix to a soft dough with the milk.

3. Roll the dough into small balls the size of a walnut and drop them into the simmering fruit. Cover the pan and simmer gently for 5 minutes until the dumplings are puffed up and cooked through. Serve immediately with single cream.

Red Fruit Compote with Cardamom Dumplings.

LEMON CURD SOUFFLÉ

Serves 4

Only make this simple soufflé if you have a really good lemon curd to use as the base, otherwise it will be bland and disappointing.

225 g (8 oz) good-quality lemon curd	a little melted butter and caster sugar for the dish
4 egg whites	icing sugar for dusting
25 g (1 oz) caster sugar	

1. Preheat the oven to 190°C (375°F, Gas Mark 5). Brush a 1.2 litre (2 pint) soufflé dish with melted butter and dust with caster sugar. Place the lemon curd in a small pan and heat gently to warm through.

2. Whisk the egg whites until stiff but not dry and then whisk in the sugar. Continue whisking for 30 seconds until stiff and glossy. Stir a spoonful of the egg white into the lemon curd, then spoon the lemon curd into the remaining egg white and fold together gently until just combined.

3. Pour the soufflé mixture into the prepared dish and bake for 20–25 minutes until well risen and golden. Dust the top with icing sugar and serve immediately.

FRESH PEACH AND ALMOND CAKE

Serves 6

This cake is wonderful served warm with clotted cream or really good vanilla ice cream. Make it with very ripe fresh peaches or apricots; out of season it is almost as good with canned fruit, and I have had success with rhubarb, too.

225 g (8 oz) self-raising flour	½ teaspoon almond essence
1 teaspoon baking powder	150 g (5 oz) butter, melted
175 g (6 oz) caster sugar	3 ripe peaches, skinned, stoned and sliced
25 g (1 oz) ground almonds	15 g (½ oz) amaretti biscuits, crushed
2 eggs	

1. Preheat the oven to 170°C (325°F, Gas Mark 3). Sift the flour and baking powder into a mixing bowl and stir in the sugar and ground almonds. Beat the eggs with the almond essence and stir into the dry ingredients with the melted butter. Beat well.

2. Spoon half the mixture into a greased loose-bottomed deep 20 cm (8 in) round cake tin. Arrange the peach slices over the top. Drop the rest of the mixture in spoonfuls over the peaches and sprinkle with the crushed amaretti biscuits.

3. Bake for 1½ hours until golden and firm to the touch. Cool in the tin for 10 minutes, then turn out on to a plate and serve warm.

POACHED PEARS IN GINGER WINE

Serves 4

We have a pear tree in the garden that produces copious quantities of fruit (which normally falls just when we're away on our summer holidays!). As a result I've been expanding my pear cookery repertoire and this is one of the experiments that have been a success.

50 g (2 oz) granulated sugar	*juice of 1 lemon*
150 ml (¼ pint) ginger wine	*4 large ripe pears*
1 stick lemon grass	

1. Place the sugar in a deep pan that will be just wide enough to hold all the pears standing up. Add 150 ml (¼ pint) water and heat gently until the sugar dissolves. Bring to the boil and simmer for 5 minutes until syrupy, then stir in the ginger wine, lemon grass and lemon juice.

2. Peel the pears and stand them in the syrup. Cover and simmer gently for 45 minutes until the pears are tender, then transfer them to a warmed serving dish. Boil the syrup rapidly until reduced by half and pour it over the pears. Serve with crème fraîche or Greek-style yoghurt.

Warm Chocolate Cake with Cinnamon Mascarpone

Serves 6–8

This almost-flourless cake has been one of my standbys since the recipe came my way when I was working at Woman and Home *magazine. It comes from near Lourdes in the French Pyrénées and I have served it in all kinds of ways over the years. It is equally delicious warm or cold, and more like a mousse than a cake. Use chocolate with a high proportion of cocoa solids (at least 50 per cent) for a really good flavour.*

175 g (6 oz) good-quality plain chocolate	FOR THE CINNAMON MASCARPONE
175 g (6 oz) unsalted butter, diced	175 g (6 oz) mascarpone cheese
4 eggs, separated	1 tablespoon caster sugar
175 g (6 oz) caster sugar	½ teaspoon ground cinnamon
2 tablespoons plain flour	2 tablespoons semi-skimmed milk
cocoa powder for dusting	

1. Preheat the oven to 180°C (350°F, Gas Mark 4). Break up the chocolate, put it in a small pan with the butter and heat gently until melted. Leave to cool.

2. Place the egg yolks and caster sugar in a large mixing bowl and whisk with an electric mixer until very pale and thick. Whisk in the melted chocolate mixture.

3. In a separate bowl, whisk the egg whites until stiff. Fold them lightly into the chocolate mixture with the flour. Pour into a greased and base-lined 23 cm (9 in) round cake tin (preferably one with sloping sides) and bake for 40–45 minutes until risen and just set.

4. While the cake is baking, prepare the mascarpone. Place the mascarpone cheese in a bowl and stir in the sugar, cinnamon and milk until well combined. Transfer to a small serving dish.

5. Cool the cake in the tin for a minute then carefully turn it out on to a wire rack (it will sink dramatically – don't worry, it's meant to). Dust with cocoa powder and serve warm with the cinnamon mascarpone.

Cold Desserts

$\mathcal{W}$HEN DECIDING how to divide up the recipes for this book I found myself automatically differentiating between hot puddings and cold desserts. For me, this seemed a natural division as my hot puds tend to fall into the comforting, warming category, while the latter are elegant, luxurious showstoppers for when I'm really out to impress. Whereas I used to go to town with the piping bag and come up with all kinds of elaborate creations, nowadays, with far more demands on my time, I prefer to let the ingredients do all the work. A sumptuous chocolate cake, rich ice cream or fresh fruit tart are all ideal for a grand finale, but they rely on the best-quality ingredients for their impact, so don't skimp on good chocolate, fresh cream and the best of the season's berries.

None of these recipes is very complicated to prepare and you need no special skills. To cut down on fat I substitute half Greek yoghurt for double cream, which works well in any dish that doesn't need heating.

MINTED MANGO FOOL

Serves 4

*Make sure the mango is really ripe for this fool. You can freeze the fool to make a delicious
ice cream. Stir it several times during freezing to prevent ice crystals forming.*

1 large ripe mango	*1 tablespoon chopped fresh mint*
150 ml (¼ pint) double cream	*1 tablespoon caster sugar (optional)*
150 ml (¼ pint) Greek-style yoghurt	*very finely shredded lime rind to decorate*
juice of ½ lime	

1. Cut the mango flesh away from the stone, then peel and cut it into cubes. Mash or
purée in a blender or food processor until smooth.

2. Lightly whip the cream until floppy, then stir in the yoghurt. Stir in the lime juice,
mint and mango purée, with the sugar if using; mix only lightly for a marbled effect.

3. Spoon the fool into long-stemmed glasses and decorate with lime rind. Chill until
ready to serve.

ORANGE AND WHISKY SYLLABUB

Serves 4

Serve this rich dessert in long-stemmed glasses for maximum effect.

4 large oranges	*3–4 tablespoons whisky*
juice of ½ lemon	*300 ml (½ pint) double cream*
75 g (3 oz) caster sugar	*finely shredded orange rind to decorate*

1. Finely grate the rind of 1 orange and squeeze the juice. Peel the other oranges
with a serrated knife, removing all the white pith, and cut them into segments, discarding any pips. Arrange in four individual serving glasses.

2. Mix together the orange and lemon juice, orange rind, sugar and whisky. Whip
the cream until floppy, then gradually beat in the juice mixture, adding it a little at a
time and beating constantly so that the cream stays thick. Pour the syllabub over the
orange segments and chill until ready to serve. Decorate with shreds of orange rind
and serve with sponge fingers or French madeleines.

Christmas Rice

I have a Swedish aunt, Anna, and just before Christmas every year we have a family get-together where she prepares an enormous spread of traditional Swedish Christmas dishes. All designed to keep out the cold, they provide an excellent base for the frequent toasts of aquavit washed down with lager that punctuate the meal. And, as you may well imagine, after such a feast the Swedish tradition of singing at the table is one we all follow with enthusiasm! The evening begins with a cup of Glögg, a mulled red wine cup spiced and served with almonds and raisins, and is often rounded off with this excellent rice dish. It is a whole world away from our own nursery rice pudding and, served with a red fruit compote, it makes a luxurious end to any meal, whatever the season.

600 ml (1 pint) milk	*25 g (1 oz) caster sugar*
1 vanilla pod	*1–2 tablespoons cherry brandy*
100 g (4 oz) pudding rice	*150 ml (¼ pint) double cream, lightly whipped*
50 g (2 oz) blanched almonds, chopped	*silver and gold dragées to decorate*

1. Put the milk in a heavy-based saucepan with the vanilla pod and bring to the boil. Add the rice and cook over a medium heat for 5 minutes, stirring frequently, then cover and simmer for 25 minutes until the mixture is thick and the rice tender. Remove the vanilla pod, transfer the rice to a bowl, cover and leave to cool.

2. Stir the almonds, sugar and cherry brandy into the rice and then fold in the whipped cream. Chill until ready to serve. Pile the rice into a shallow glass serving dish and decorate with the dragées.

FRESH RASPBERRY TART

Fresh British raspberries are my favourite soft fruit. At the start of the season all they need is a spoonful of double cream to make the perfect end to a meal. Later on I use them to make this tart, which is equally delicious warm or cold. For a special occasion you could make the mixture into little tartlets.

	For the filling
175 g (6 oz) plain flour	
75 g (3 oz) unsalted butter at room temperature, diced	150 ml (¼ pint) crème fraîche
	125 ml (4 fl oz) Greek-style yoghurt
50 g (2 oz) caster sugar	50 g (2 oz) caster sugar
1 egg, beaten	2 eggs
	225 g (8 oz) fresh raspberries

1. Preheat the oven to 200°C (400°F, Gas Mark 6). Sift the flour on to a clean work surface and make a well in the centre. Put the butter, sugar and egg in the well and work together with your fingertips to form a stiff dough. Knead lightly until smooth, then wrap and chill for 30 minutes.

2. Roll out the pastry and use to line a 25 cm (10 in) loose-bottomed flan tin. Line with crumpled greaseproof paper and fill with baking beans. Bake for 10 minutes, then remove the beans and paper.

3. Beat together the crème fraîche, yoghurt, sugar and eggs. Arrange the raspberries in the pastry case and pour over the cream and egg mixture.

4. Reduce the oven temperature to 180°C (350°F, Gas Mark 4). Bake the tart for 35 minutes until the filling is set and golden. Leave to cool, then serve.

AMARETTI AND CHOCOLATE CAKE

Serves 6–8

This is halfway between a cake and a mousse, and a little goes a very long way. Use the best-quality chocolate you can find – one with at least 50 per cent cocoa solids – to ensure a really chocolatey flavour; it's just not worth making it with inferior chocolate. Look out for amaretti biscuits in Italian delicatessens or large supermarkets, or use macaroons instead.

175 g (6 oz) good-quality plain chocolate	To finish
2 tablespoons brandy or grappa	3–4 tablespoons apricot jam
175 g (6 oz) unsalted butter	150 g (5 oz) mascarpone cheese
175 g (6 oz) caster sugar	about 2 tablespoons milk
4 eggs, separated	icing sugar for dusting
75 g (3 oz) amaretti biscuits, crushed	
75 g (3 oz) plain flour, sifted	

1. Preheat the oven to 180°C (350°F, Gas Mark 4). Grease and line a 23 cm (9 in) round cake tin (preferably one with sloping sides). Break up the chocolate and place it with the brandy or grappa in a bowl set over a pan of gently simmering water. Stir until melted.

2. Cream the butter with the sugar until pale and fluffy, then beat in the egg yolks one at a time. Stir in the melted chocolate, then fold in the crushed amaretti and the flour.

3. Whisk the egg whites until stiff, then fold them quickly and lightly into the chocolate mixture. Spoon into the prepared cake tin and smooth the surface.

4. Bake for 40–45 minutes until just firm to the touch but still slightly sticky in the centre. Cool in the tin for 10 minutes, then turn out carefully on to a wire rack and leave to cool. This cake is very crumbly and delicate so handle it with care.

5. To serve, carefully cut the cake in half with a serrated knife and spread the bottom half with the apricot jam. Mix the mascarpone with enough milk to give a spreading consistency and spread it over the jam. Put the top half of the cake back in position and dust with icing sugar.

ROSE PETAL MERINGUE CAKE

Serves 6

This is really just a pavlova decorated with frosted rose petals but it's always a great success with summer guests. Sometimes I make the meringue with rose petal sugar for a really over-the-top flavour. If you want to try this, simply place 225 g (8 oz) caster sugar in a blender with 6–8 freshly washed rose petals (choose a highly scented variety) and whizz until finely ground. Store in an airtight container for up to one month.

4 egg whites at room temperature	about 12 pale and dark pink rose petals
225 g (8 oz) caster sugar	3 tablespoons caster sugar
½ teaspoon cornflour	350 g (12 oz) mixed red fruit, such as raspberries,
½ teaspoon white wine vinegar	strawberries, currants, cherries and blueberries
	150 ml (¼ pint) double cream, lightly whipped
For the filling	150 ml (¼ pint) Greek-style yoghurt
1 egg white	1 tablespoon crème de cassis (optional)

1. Preheat the oven to 140°C (275°F, Gas Mark 1). Line a baking sheet with baking parchment and draw a 20 cm (8 in) circle on it, using a plate or a tin as a guide. Place the egg whites in a clean mixing bowl and whisk until stiff. Gradually whisk in half the caster sugar and continue whisking until very stiff and glossy. Gently fold in the rest of the sugar, plus the cornflour and vinegar.

2. Spread half the meringue evenly over the marked circle. Drop spoonfuls of the remaining meringue round the edge to form a border. Bake for 1½–2 hours until set and very pale golden. Turn off the oven and leave the meringue in it to cool.

3. To frost the rose petals, lightly whisk the egg white with a fork, then dip each rose petal in it and then into the caster sugar to coat. Leave on a sheet of baking parchment to dry.

4. To assemble the meringue cake, wash the fruit, hull the strawberries and stone the cherries. Stir together the whipped cream, yoghurt and crème de cassis if using. Remove the meringue from the baking parchment and place on a serving dish, then fill with the cream. Just before serving, pile the fruit and rose petals on top.

Hazelnut Roulade with Raspberries and Redcurrants

Serves 6

The classic pairing of hazelnuts and raspberries is used to great effect in this fresh-tasting roulade. It freezes well so is ideal for entertaining large numbers.

3 eggs, separated	*For the filling*
100 g (4 oz) caster sugar	*150 ml (¼ pint) double cream, lightly whipped*
50 g (2 oz) hazelnuts, toasted and ground	*100 g (4 oz) fresh raspberries*
15 g (½ oz) semolina	*50 g (2 oz) fresh redcurrants*
	icing sugar for dusting
	extra raspberries and redcurrants and fresh mint
	leaves to decorate

1. Preheat the oven to 170°C (325°F, Gas Mark 3). Place the egg yolks in a mixing bowl with the sugar and whisk with an electric mixer until really thick and pale. Fold in the ground hazelnuts and semolina. In a separate bowl, whisk the egg whites until stiff and then gently fold them into the hazelnut mixture.

2. Spoon the mixture into a greased and lined 20 x 30 cm (8 x 12 in) Swiss roll tin and level the surface. Bake for 20–25 minutes until golden. Leave to cool in the tin, covered with a damp tea towel.

3. To assemble, turn the roulade out on to a sheet of baking parchment and peel off the lining paper. Trim the edges neatly and spread with the whipped cream. Scatter the fruit over the cream and carefully roll up the roulade, using the baking parchment to help support the cake.

4. Transfer the roulade to a plate and chill until ready to serve. Just before serving, dust with icing sugar and decorate with raspberries, redcurrants and fresh mint leaves.

BRANDY ICE CREAM

Serves 6

I make this ice cream at Christmas to serve with the pudding and mince pies but it is very good at any time of year. The method makes it useful for anyone in a hurry, since it doesn't need beating during the freezing process yet it still has a creamy, luxurious texture. It is well worth searching out really high-quality candied fruit but you could use glacé fruit if pushed.

100 g (4 oz) candied fruit, chopped	1 vanilla pod
5 tablespoons brandy	5 egg yolks
75 g (3 oz) caster sugar	600 ml (1 pint) double cream

1. Place the fruit and brandy in a small bowl and leave to stand overnight.

2. The next day, place the sugar and vanilla pod in a small, heavy-based pan with 150 ml (¼ pint) water. Heat very gently until the sugar dissolves, then bring to the boil and continue boiling until the syrup reaches 110°C (230°F) when tested with a sugar thermometer or reaches the thread stage (to test this, place 1 teaspoon of the syrup on a saucer; when cooled it should create a thin thread if pressed between finger and thumb). Remove the pan from the heat and leave to cool for a minute, then remove the vanilla pod.

3. Place the egg yolks in a large mixing bowl and gradually pour in the hot sugar syrup, whisking constantly. Continue whisking until the mixture is very pale, thick and cool.

4. Beat the cream until floppy, then fold it into the egg mixture with the soaked fruit and brandy. Pour into a rigid container and freeze for about 4 hours or until firm. Transfer the ice cream to the fridge for 15 minutes before serving to soften.

BRANDY ICE CREAM SERVED WITH HAZELNUT AND LEMON BISCOTTI (SEE PAGE 152).

Hazelnut and Lemon Biscotti

Makes 10

In Italy these little biscuits are served at the end of a meal with a glass of fortified dessert wine, Vin Santo. *Traditionally made with almonds, they are available in Italian delicatessens but are very simple to make at home. My biscuits are made with hazelnuts and taste wonderful with ice creams and fruit fools (see preceding page).*

100 g (4 oz) plain flour	*75 g (3 oz) toasted hazelnuts, roughly chopped*
¼ teaspoon baking powder	*grated rind of ½ lemon*
75 g (3 oz) caster sugar	*1 egg, beaten*

1. Preheat the oven to 200°C (400°F, Gas Mark 6). Sift the flour and baking powder into a bowl and stir in the sugar, hazelnuts and lemon rind. Work in the egg to give a firm dough.

2. Turn the dough on to a lightly floured work surface and roll into a long sausage about 23 cm (9 in) long. Transfer to a non-stick baking sheet and bake for about 25 minutes until pale golden.

3. Remove the baking sheet from the oven and cut the biscuit mixture on the diagonal into 10. Arrange the biscuits cut side down on the baking sheet and return to the oven for a further 10 minutes until golden. Transfer to a wire rack to cool. Store in an air-tight container for up to 10 days.

LEMON-SOAKED ALMOND CAKE

Serves 6

Ground almonds give this cake a moist texture that is an ideal foil for fresh tart fruit.
In the winter serve it with sliced oranges.

100 g (4 oz) unsalted butter	TO FINISH
100 g (4 oz) caster sugar	juice of 1 lemon
grated rind and juice of 1 lemon	75 g (3 oz) granulated sugar
2 eggs, separated	fresh raspberries and blueberries
100 g (4 oz) ground almonds	
40 g (1½ oz) plain flour, sifted	

1. Preheat the oven to 180°C (350°F, Gas Mark 4). Cream the butter with the sugar and lemon rind until pale and fluffy. Beat in the egg yolks one at a time. Fold in the ground almonds and sifted flour with the lemon juice. In a separate bowl, stiffly whisk the egg whites and fold them gently into the mixture.

2. Spoon the mixture into a greased and base-lined 18 cm (7 in) round cake tin and level the surface. Bake for 30–35 minutes until golden and firm to the touch.

3. While the cake is cooking, mix the lemon juice with the granulated sugar. As soon as the cake comes out of the oven, pour the lemon syrup over it. Leave to cool in the tin for 10 minutes, then turn out on to a wire rack and leave to cool completely. Serve with fresh raspberries and blueberries.

CHOCOLATE RASPBERRY TERRINE

Serves 6–8

The easiest way to cut this layered terrine is with a warm knife.

2 eggs	90 ml (3 fl oz) boiling water
50 g (2 oz) caster sugar	225 g (8 oz) fresh raspberries
few drops of natural vanilla essence	chocolate curls, extra raspberries and
40 g (1½ oz) plain flour	cocoa powder to decorate
1 tablespoon cocoa powder	
25 g (1 oz) butter, melted and cooled	FOR THE CHOCOLATE MOUSSE
2 tablespoons brandy	175 g (6 oz) good-quality plain chocolate
1 teaspoon instant coffee granules dissolved in	300 ml (½ pint) double cream, lightly whipped

1. Preheat the oven to 190°C (375°F, Gas Mark 5). Place the eggs, sugar and vanilla essence in a mixing bowl and whisk with an electric mixer until very thick and pale. Sift the flour and cocoa powder over the surface and fold in quickly and lightly, then fold in the melted butter. Pour into a greased and lined 8 x 30 cm (3 x 12 in) loaf tin – it will only just half fill it – and bake for 25–30 minutes until well risen and firm to the touch. Turn out on to a wire rack to cool.

2. To make the mousse, break up the chocolate and place in a small bowl set over a pan of simmering water. Stir until melted, then cool slightly. Whisk half the cooled chocolate into the cream and then fold in the remainder with a metal spoon.

3. To assemble the terrine, cut the cake in half horizontally and place one half back in the loaf tin. Mix the brandy and coffee together and sprinkle half over the cake in the tin. Spread the raspberries over the cake and top with the chocolate mousse. Level the surface and arrange the other half of the cake on top. Sprinkle with the rest of the brandy and coffee.

4. Cover the terrine with foil and chill for several hours. To serve, run a knife that has been dipped in hot water around the edges of the terrine, then turn it out on to a serving plate. Arrange chocolate curls and raspberries on top and dust with cocoa powder.

CHOCOLATE RASPBERRY TERRINE.

Rhubarb Fool with Ginger Shortbread Hearts

Serves 4

*I love rhubarb, especially in a fool. Make the shortbread into heart shapes and serve this as
a romantic dessert on Valentine's Day.*

680 g (1½ lb) rhubarb, cut into chunks	FOR THE SHORTBREAD
75 g (3 oz) caster sugar	100 g (4 oz) butter
150 ml (¼ pint) double cream	50 g (2 oz) caster sugar
1 teaspoon cornflour	50 g (2 oz) rice flour or ground rice
2 egg yolks	125 g (4½ oz) plain flour
few drops of natural vanilla essence	40 g (1½ oz) preserved stem ginger,
150 ml (¼ pint) Greek-style yoghurt	finely chopped
	extra caster sugar for sprinkling

1. First make the shortbread. Preheat the oven to 150°C (300°F, Gas Mark 2).
Cream the butter until very soft and light, then gradually beat in the caster sugar and
continue beating until light and fluffy. Work in the flours with the ginger and knead
lightly to form a stiff dough. Chill for 15 minutes, then roll out to about 1 cm (½ in)
thick and cut out heart shapes with a metal biscuit cutter. Re-roll the trimmings and
cut out more biscuits.

2. Place the biscuits on a baking sheet and bake for 20–25 minutes until pale golden
and crisp. Sprinkle with caster sugar and leave to cool on the baking sheet. Store in
an airtight container for up to 3 weeks.

3. To make the fool, place the rhubarb in a pan with 50 g (2 oz) of the caster sugar,
cover and cook over a very gentle heat for 15–20 minutes, stirring occasionally, until
the rhubarb is tender. Leave to cool, then purée in a blender or food processor.

4. Put the cream in a small pan and heat to boiling point. In a bowl, whisk together
the cornflour, egg yolks, vanilla essence and remaining sugar. Pour on the cream,
whisking continuously, then pour the mixture back into the pan and heat gently
until thickened, stirring all the time. Cool, then fold it together with the Greek
yoghurt and rhubarb purée. Spoon the fool into serving glasses or dishes and chill.
Serve with the ginger shortbread.

Festive and Party Food

SPECIAL OCCASIONS provide a wonderful opportunity for cooks to show off. I love entertaining for larger parties – with a little thought and forward planning they need not be much more trouble than the average dinner party, as long as you pick the right dishes. By balancing flavours, colours and textures it's very easy to devise a striking menu that will satisfy both meat eaters and vegetarians alike; I find such occasions a great way of showing sceptics just how stunning such a spread can be. Don't make a point out of the food being vegetarian, let it speak for itself.

When entertaining large numbers, try to plan a menu that combines the simple with the more elaborate, and make full use of some of the excellent ready-prepared foods now available in our shops. Then you won't be too burdened with preparation and can really put an effort into the key dishes. Choose two main dishes, one uncomplicated and one more adventurous – this works well for both the cook and the guests. Serve baskets of interesting breads, a selection of simple salads (I usually do a leafy green one, a red one and a pasta- or rice-based one), and then add a couple of dishes that will get people talking. Use an unusual ingredient, search out something that people may have heard of but are unlikely to have tried. This could be anything from a new bread to a local speciality – for information on how to find such foods I recommend Henrietta Green's *Food Lover's Guide to Britain* (BBC Books). Finally, serve one spectacular pudding – I always used to feel I had to offer a selection but have now realized that this only makes more work and people don't need the choice. Fruit and interesting cheeses round off the meal very nicely.

Above all, remember that food is the catalyst that brings people together and gets them talking. Parties should be enjoyed by the giver as well as the guests.

SESAME CHEESE ROLLS

Makes 20

These are my version of the veggie sausage roll, and I think they make a great alternative to some of the greasy offerings served up at parties. They are also popular in my children's school lunchboxes.

100 g (4 oz) Cheddar, grated	*1 egg*
1 small onion, grated	*1 egg yolk*
150 g (5 oz) fresh brown breadcrumbs	*225 g (8 oz) puff pastry, thawed if frozen*
40 g (1½ oz) walnut pieces, finely chopped	*salt and freshly ground black pepper*
1 tablespoon sesame seeds	*beaten egg to glaze*
½ teaspoon mustard powder	*sesame seeds for sprinkling*

1. Preheat the oven to 220°C (425°F, Gas Mark 7). Place the cheese, onion, breadcrumbs, walnuts, sesame seeds and mustard powder in a bowl and mix well, then season to taste. Beat the egg and egg yolk together and stir into the dry ingredients to bind.

2. Roll out the pastry to a 45 x 23 cm (18 x 9 in) rectangle and cut it in half lengthways. Spoon the filling down the centre of each sheet of pastry and shape into a long sausage. Brush the edges of the pastry with water, then fold them over the filling and press the edges together to seal.

3. Cut into 4 cm (1½ in) lengths and transfer to greased baking sheets. Brush with beaten egg and sprinkle with sesame seeds. Bake the rolls for 15 minutes until golden, then cool on a wire rack. Serve warm.

Stilton, Leek and Pear Tarts

Makes 12 tartlets

I use a cheesy pastry to make these tarts but ready-made shortcrust also works well. They make great nibbles or you could make larger ones in individual tart tins to serve as a starter.

	For the filling
175 g (6 oz) plain flour	*15 g (½ oz) butter*
pinch each of salt and cayenne pepper	*1 small leek, shredded*
75 g (3 oz) butter	*75 g (3 oz) Stilton cheese, crumbled*
25 g (1 oz) strong Cheddar, grated	*2 egg yolks*
1 egg yolk	*200 ml (7 fl oz) single cream*
	1 large ripe pear, peeled, cored and sliced
	salt and freshly ground black pepper

1. Sift the flour, salt and cayenne into a mixing bowl and rub in the butter until the mixture resembles breadcrumbs. Stir in the Cheddar. Mix the egg yolk with 2 tablespoons cold water, add to the dry ingredients and mix to a firm dough with a knife. Knead lightly until smooth, then wrap and chill for 10 minutes.

2. Preheat the oven to 190°C (375°F, Gas Mark 5). Melt the butter in a small pan and cook the leek gently for 5 minutes until softened. Leave to cool. Roll out the pastry and use to line 12 tartlet tins.

3. Divide the leek between the tarts and sprinkle over the Stilton. Mix the egg yolks with the cream and seasoning and pour into the tarts. Cut the pear slices in half and arrange them on top.

4. Bake the tartlets for 20 minutes until puffy and golden. Serve warm.

Vegetable Samosas

Samosas are ideal for entertaining because you can make them in advance and heat them through, vary them in size to serve as finger food or a starter, and use almost anything for the filling. Play around with this basic recipe as you wish but make sure you use a good-quality curry paste to ensure a good flavour.

225 g (8 oz) potato	*100 g (4 oz) frozen mixed vegetables,*
1 tablespoon sunflower oil	*thawed*
½ teaspoon cumin seeds	*1 tablespoon lemon juice*
1 small onion, finely chopped	*salt*
1 garlic clove, crushed	*4 large sheets filo pastry*
1 teaspoon mild curry paste	*25 g (1 oz) butter, melted*

1. Preheat the oven to 200°C (400°F, Gas Mark 6). Cook the potato in simmering water until tender, then drain and cool. Peel and cut into small dice.

2. Heat the oil in a frying pan, add the cumin seeds and cook for 30 seconds, then add the onion and garlic and stir over a medium heat for 5 minutes until lightly browned. Stir in the curry paste and cook for 1 minute. Add the potato, vegetables, lemon juice and salt and mix well.

3. Cut each sheet of filo into four long strips, place a teaspoonful of the filling at the top of each strip and fold down one corner to make a triangle. Continue folding down the strip to make a neat parcel.

4. Place the samosas on a greased baking sheet, brush with the melted butter and bake for 10–12 minutes until crisp and golden. Serve warm.

Mushroom and Thyme Raised Pie

Serves 8–10

This is a version of a pie I made for a feature in BBC Vegetarian Good Food, *which has proved an enormous success with vegetarians and meat eaters alike every time I have made it. It's ideal for entertaining and for summer picnics, sliced in wedges and served with a good home-made chutney.*

225 g (8 oz) plain flour	450 g (1 lb) chestnut mushrooms, chopped
225 g (8 oz) wholemeal flour	450 g (1 lb) carrots, coarsely grated
1 teaspoon salt	175 g (6 oz) wholemeal breadcrumbs
50 g (2 oz) white vegetable fat, diced	50 g (2 oz) mature Cheddar, grated
3 tablespoons olive oil	2 tablespoons chopped fresh thyme
125 ml (4 fl oz) semi-skimmed milk	large pinch of cayenne pepper
	100 g (4 oz) feta cheese, crumbled
FOR THE FILLING	10 large fresh basil leaves, chopped
2 tablespoons olive oil	8 stoned black olives, chopped
1 large onion, chopped	salt and freshly ground black pepper
2 garlic cloves, crushed	

1. Preheat the oven to 180°C (350°F, Gas Mark 4). First prepare the filling. Heat the oil in a large frying pan and cook the onion and garlic for 3 minutes until softened. Add the mushrooms and cook, stirring, over a medium heat for 5 minutes until softened.

2. Place the carrots, breadcrumbs, Cheddar, thyme, cayenne and seasoning in a bowl, add the mushroom mixture and stir until thoroughly combined. In a separate bowl mix the feta, basil and olives together.

3. To make the pastry, put the flours and salt in a large mixing bowl. Place the white fat, olive oil and milk in a small pan with 150 ml (¼ pint) water and heat gently until the fat melts. Add to the dry ingredients and mix to a soft dough. Turn on to a lightly floured work surface and knead lightly until smooth.

4. Roll out two-thirds of the pastry and use to line a deep 20 cm (8 in) loose-bottomed cake tin. Spoon in half the carrot and mushroom mixture and spread level. Scatter the feta mixture over the top, then add the rest of the filling and press down lightly.

5. Roll out the remaining pastry and use to cover the pie, pinching the edges together to seal. Make a steam hole in the centre and use the pastry trimmings to decorate. Bake the pie for 1¼–1½ hours, covering the top with foil if it gets too brown. Cool in the tin, then chill until ready to serve.

Moroccan Filo Pie

Serves 6

North African food frequently mixes sweet with savoury and the original inspiration for this pie is finished off with a dusting of icing sugar and cinnamon. I find that people expect a sweet interior with such a decoration, so I prefer to keep the spicing to the inside of the dish and omit the sugar.

4 eggs	2 tablespoons chopped fresh flat-leaf parsley
1 large red pepper	50 g (2 oz) blanched almonds
15 g (½ oz) dried porcini mushrooms	225 g (8 oz) chestnut mushrooms, sliced
¼ teaspoon saffron strands	225 g (8 oz) carrots, coarsely grated
50 g (2 oz) butter	1 bunch watercress, chopped
1 large onion, finely chopped	9 large sheets filo pastry
1 teaspoon ground cinnamon	salt and freshly ground black pepper
large pinch each of ground ginger and allspice	

1. Preheat the oven to 180°C (350°F, Gas Mark 4). Place the eggs in a pan of cold water, bring to the boil and simmer for 8 minutes. Cool under running water, then shell. Grill the pepper on all sides until blackened, then place in a plastic bag for a few minutes to loosen the skin. Pour 150 ml (¼ pint) hot water over the porcini and leave to stand for 15 minutes. Drain, reserving the liquid. Soak the saffron in 2 tablespoons boiling water for 5 minutes.

2. Heat half the butter in a large frying pan, add the onion and cook for 5 minutes until softened. Add the saffron with its liquid, plus the spices, parsley, mushroom liquid and seasoning, and simmer for 10–15 minutes until the liquid has almost evaporated.

3. Chop the eggs coarsely and stir them into the onion mixture. Dry fry the almonds in a clean frying pan until golden, then chop them and add to the egg mixture.

4. Slice the soaked mushrooms and mix them with the chestnut mushrooms, carrot and watercress. Skin, deseed and chop the red pepper and add to the mushroom mixture.

Moroccan Filo Pie.

5. Melt the remaining butter and brush two sheets of filo with it, then use them to line a 23 cm (9 in) loose-bottomed cake tin, leaving the edges hanging over the sides. Fold another sheet of filo in half, brush with butter and use to line the base of the tin.

6. Spread the onion and egg mixture over the pastry and cover with another sheet of filo, folded in half. Spoon over the carrot and mushroom mixture and top with four sheets of filo, tucking the edges neatly in all round the sides. Brush the top of the pie with melted butter. Cut the remaining sheet of filo into strips, crumple them up and arrange over the top of the pie. Drizzle over any remaining butter.

7. Bake for 40–45 minutes until golden and crisp. Serve with Quick Lemon Hollandaise (see page 187).

Non-vegetarian Tip

STIR 225 G (8 OZ) DICED COOKED CHICKEN OR PHEASANT INTO THE ONION MIXTURE AND PROCEED AS ABOVE.

Spiced Red Cabbage with Cranberries

Serves 4

This cabbage dish is delicious both hot and cold and goes well with the croustades on pages 73 and 170.

1 tablespoon sunflower oil	1 eating apple, cored and diced
1 large onion, thinly sliced	1 tablespoon light muscovado sugar
1 teaspoon ground coriander	5 tablespoons red wine vinegar
½ teaspoon ground cinnamon	100 g (4 oz) fresh cranberries
¼ teaspoon freshly grated nutmeg	2 tablespoons redcurrant jelly
680 g (1½ lb) red cabbage, shredded	salt and freshly ground black pepper

1. Heat the oil in a large pan, add the onion and cook for 3 minutes over a medium heat until softened. Stir in the spices and cook for a further minute, then add the cabbage and continue cooking for 2 minutes until just beginning to wilt.

2. Stir in the apple, sugar, vinegar, seasoning and 150 ml (¼ pint) water and bring to the boil. Cover and simmer for 1 hour, stirring occasionally, until the cabbage is tender. Add more water if the mixture gets too dry.

3. Stir in the cranberries and redcurrant jelly and simmer for a further 10 minutes until the cranberries pop. Check the seasoning and serve.

CHESTNUT AND CRANBERRY CASSEROLE WITH PORT

Serves 6

Fresh chestnuts have an infinitely better flavour and texture than canned so it is well worth buying them if you can be bothered to peel them. I've started to use them far more since someone told me to put them in the microwave for a few minutes to loosen the skins, which works a dream. Simply pierce the chestnuts with a knife, then cook them four at a time on High for 1 minute until the skins split. They will peel easily.

3 tablespoons olive oil	1 bay leaf
350 g (12 oz) shallots or button onions, peeled (see page 37)	½ teaspoon ground mace
	½ teaspoon ground cloves
350 g (12 oz) carrots, sliced	salt and freshly ground black pepper
2 celery sticks, sliced	300 ml (½ pint) red wine
2 garlic cloves, chopped	150 ml (¼ pint) vegetable stock (see page 186)
680 g (1½ lb) fresh chestnuts, peeled	225 g (8 oz) fresh cranberries
1 tablespoon plain flour	4 tablespoons port
grated rind and juice of 1 orange	chopped fresh parsley and finely shredded
3 tablespoons chopped fresh flat-leaf parsley	orange rind to garnish
1 tablespoon chopped fresh thyme	

1. Heat the oil in a flameproof casserole and cook the shallots or button onions over a medium heat until golden. Remove from the pan with a slotted spoon. Add the carrots, celery, garlic and chestnuts to the pan and cook, stirring, for about 8 minutes until golden.

2. Return the shallots to the pan with the flour and cook for 1 minute. Stir in the orange rind and juice, parsley, thyme, bay leaf, spices and seasoning, then pour in the wine and stock. Bring to the boil, then cover and simmer for 35–40 minutes until the vegetables are almost tender.

3. Stir in the cranberries and port and simmer for a further 20 minutes. Garnish with chopped parsley and shredded orange rind and serve.

Non-vegetarian Tip

REDUCE THE QUANTITY OF VEGETABLES BY HALF, ADD 680 G (1½ LB) CUBED STEWING STEAK TO THE PAN AFTER FRYING THE SHALLOTS, AND BROWN ON ALL SIDES. ADD AN EXTRA 300 ML (½ PINT) STOCK AND COOK THE CASSEROLE FOR AN EXTRA 1½ HOURS UNTIL THE MEAT IS TENDER. FINISH AS ABOVE.

PINE NUT AND PEPPER TERRINE

Serves 6–8

When I first became editor of BBC Vegetarian Good Food *I promised myself I would
never feature a recipe for that old chestnut, the nut roast. I changed my mind when Sophie
Grigson came up with a wonderful recipe based on pine nuts, which we ran in the
magazine with great success. This is my tribute to that recipe, which I think originated
from the Carved Angel restaurant in Dartmouth. It is delicious both hot and cold so
I usually make up double quantities and freeze one to serve later.*

2 red peppers	*2 tablespoons chopped fresh parsley*
2 yellow peppers	*2 tablespoons chopped fresh basil*
2 green peppers	*1 tablespoon toasted sesame seeds*
3 tablespoons extra virgin olive oil	*freshly grated nutmeg*
1 onion, chopped	*2 eggs, beaten*
100 g (4 oz) pine nuts, chopped	*15 g (½ oz) ground almonds*
100 g (4 oz) blanched almonds, chopped	*salt and freshly ground black pepper*
100 g (4 oz) fresh white breadcrumbs	*fresh watercress to garnish*

1. Preheat the oven to 200°C (400°F, Gas Mark 6). Place all the peppers on a baking
sheet and bake for 15–20 minutes until blackened. Transfer to a plastic bag for
5 minutes to loosen the skins. Halve, peel off the skins and deseed. Cut each pepper
half in half again to give long strips.

2. Heat the oil in a medium frying pan and cook the onion for 5 minutes until softened. Put the pine nuts, almonds and breadcrumbs in a mixing bowl. Add the herbs,
sesame seeds, cooked onion, nutmeg and seasoning and mix well. Stir in the eggs to
bind the mixture.

3. Butter a 23 x 13 cm (9 x 5 in) loaf tin and dust with the ground almonds. Spoon in
a quarter of the nut mixture and press down. Arrange a layer of red pepper strips on
top. Carry on layering the nut mixture and peppers so that you finish with a nut layer
and have three different-coloured layers of pepper.

4. Cover the tin with foil and bake for 1 hour. Turn out and garnish with fresh
watercress. Serve hot, warm or cold, with Cumberland Sauce (see page 185).

Preceding pages: QUAIL'S EGG, SAFFRON AND WILD RICE FILO WREATH (SEE OPPOSITE) SERVED
WITH SPINACH WITH RAISINS AND PINE NUTS (SEE PAGE 126) AND CREAMY CELERIAC AND SPROUT
PURÉE (SEE PAGE 171).

Quail's Egg, Saffron and Wild Rice Filo Wreath

Serves 6

This wreath makes a very festive centrepiece for the Christmas table with its herb-strewn filo leaves – I have also made it quite successfully with shortcrust pastry. It can be assembled several hours ahead, refrigerated and then cooked just before you need it. Do remember to keep the filo covered with a damp tea towel while you are working with it or it will dry out.

8 large sheets filo pastry	*½ teaspoon saffron strands*
50 g (2 oz) butter, melted	*2 tablespoons olive oil*
fresh bay leaves, rosemary and thyme sprigs to garnish	*2 shallots, finely chopped*
	50 g (2 oz) pine nuts, toasted
	2 sun-dried tomatoes in olive oil, chopped
For the filling	*3 tablespoons chopped fresh basil*
12 quail's eggs	*4 tablespoons crème fraîche*
225 g (8 oz) basmati rice	*salt and freshly ground black pepper*
350 g (12 oz) fresh spinach	

1. Preheat the oven to 200°C (400°F, Gas Mark 6). Place the quail's eggs in a pan of cold water, bring to the boil and simmer for 3 minutes. Drain and cool under cold running water, then shell.

2. Cook the rice according to the packet instructions, cool under cold running water and drain well. Blanch the spinach for a minute in boiling water, cool quickly under cold water, then drain and pat dry with kitchen paper. Soak the saffron strands in 2 tablespoons boiling water.

3. Heat the oil in a frying pan, add the shallots and cook over a medium heat for 3 minutes until softened. Remove from the heat, add the rice, saffron liquid, pine nuts, sun-dried tomatoes, basil, crème fraîche and seasoning and mix well.

4. To assemble the wreath, layer three sheets of filo on top of each other, brushing each one with melted butter. Arrange half the spinach leaves over the top two-thirds of the filo, leaving a 2.5 cm (1 in) border. Spread half the rice mixture over the spinach and place six quail's eggs along the top edge. Carefully roll up the filo, transfer to a greased baking sheet and shape into a semi-circle.

5. Repeat this process with three more sheets of filo and the rest of the filling ingredients. Tuck the pastry edges of the two semi-circles into each other to form a ring about 28 cm (11 in) in diameter.

6. Put one of the remaining filo sheets on top of the other, fold in half and cut out holly leaves with a metal cutter. Separate the leaves. Brush the wreath with melted butter and decorate with the leaves, then brush them with butter. Bake for 35–40 minutes until golden. Transfer to a warm serving dish and decorate with fresh herbs. Serve hot or cold.

CARAMELIZED CABBAGE AND GOAT'S CHEESE CROUSTADE

Serves 6

I very rarely have the time or the inclination to make pastry these days but when I do I make sure it's for a dish that will really benefit from the superior flavour and texture of home-made pastry. This recipe is made with quick flaky pastry and is well worth the effort, as it tastes just as good as it looks.

FOR THE QUICK FLAKY PASTRY	25 g (1 oz) butter
175 g (6 oz) butter	1 teaspoon caster sugar
225 g (8 oz) plain flour	½ teaspoon ground cumin
pinch of salt	1 medium onion, sliced
glass of iced water with a slice of lemon	100 g (4 oz) goat's cheese, crumbled
beaten egg to glaze	3 tablespoons freshly grated Parmesan
	4 tablespoons double cream
FOR THE FILLING	salt and freshly ground black pepper
½ small Savoy cabbage, finely shredded	

1. To make the pastry, place the block of butter in the freezer until hard. Sift the flour and salt into a bowl. Remove the butter from the freezer, wrap one end in foil and coarsely grate the butter into the flour. Stir the butter into the flour with the blade of a knife just until each piece is coated with flour. Sprinkle 3–4 tablespoons iced water over the dry ingredients and mix to a soft dough with a round-bladed knife. Finally bring it together with your hands, then wrap and chill for 30 minutes.

2. Preheat the oven to 220°C (425°F, Gas Mark 7). To prepare the filling, cook the cabbage in boiling water for a couple of minutes until wilted, then drain thoroughly. Melt half the butter in a frying pan and add the cabbage and sugar. Cook over a low heat until just tender. Stir in the cumin and seasoning. In a separate pan, cook the onion in the remaining butter for 10 minutes until golden brown.

3. Roll out half the pastry on a lightly floured work surface and cut out a 23 cm (9 in) circle, using a plate or tin as a guide. Put the pastry circle on a baking sheet and brush the edges with water. Spoon the cabbage mixture over the centre, leaving a 2.5 cm (1 in) border, then top with the onion. Crumble the goat's cheese over the top and sprinkle with the Parmesan and cream. Season well.

4. Roll out the remaining pastry to a circle just larger than the base and use to cover the filling. Seal the edges well and knock them up with the blade of a knife. Mark a lattice pattern on the top of the croustade with a knife, brush with beaten egg and bake for 20–25 minutes until the pastry is puffy and golden. Transfer to a warmed serving plate and cut into wedges to serve.

CREAMY CELERIAC AND SPROUT PURÉE

Serves 4

This delicately flavoured vegetable dish makes an excellent accompaniment to any festive main course, vegetarian or otherwise (see pages 166-67).

350 g (12 oz) Brussels sprouts	1 egg yolk
450 g (1 lb) celeriac, cubed	150 ml (¼ pint) single cream
25 g (1 oz) butter	2 tablespoons dried breadcrumbs
1 tablespoon plain flour	2 tablespoons freshly grated Parmesan
5 tablespoons milk	salt and freshly ground black pepper

1. Preheat the oven to 180°C (350°F, Gas Mark 4). Bring two pans of water to the boil and cook the Brussels sprouts in one for about 8 minutes until tender, then drain. Cook the celeriac in the other pan for 15–20 minutes until tender. Drain.

2. While the vegetables are cooking, melt the butter in a small pan, add the flour and cook for 1 minute. Gradually stir in the milk and bring to the boil, still stirring, until you have a smooth, thick sauce. Season well.

3. Place the drained vegetables in a food processor or blender with the white sauce and process until smooth. Add the egg yolk and cream and process again until combined. Check the seasoning.

4. Pour the vegetable mixture into a buttered baking dish and sprinkle with the breadcrumbs and Parmesan. Bake for 20–25 minutes until puffy and golden. Serve immediately.

REDCURRANT AND ROQUEFORT KOULIBIAC

Serves 6

Roquefort is the most expensive of blue cheeses but has a uniquely salty tang that works well with the sweet and sour flavour of redcurrants. You can substitute Stilton or another blue cheese but the results will not be quite the same.

450 g (1 lb) puff pastry, thawed if frozen	150 ml (¼ pint) dry white wine
beaten egg to glaze	150 ml (¼ pint) vegetable stock (see page 186)
	½ teaspoon chopped fresh dill
FOR THE FILLING	12 quail's eggs
25 g (1 oz) butter	1 teaspoon capers, chopped
1 small onion, chopped	100 g (4 oz) Roquefort cheese, diced
1 teaspoon grated fresh root ginger	100 g (4 oz) redcurrants, thawed if frozen
100 g (4 oz) wild and basmati rice mix	salt and freshly ground black pepper

1. First make the filling. Heat the butter in a medium pan, add the onion and ginger and cook for 3 minutes until softened. Stir in the rice and cook for a couple of minutes, then add the wine, stock, dill and seasoning and bring to the boil. Cover and simmer for 12–15 minutes until the liquid is absorbed and the rice is tender. Leave to cool.

2. Preheat the oven to 200°C (400°F, Gas Mark 6). Place the quail's eggs in a small pan, cover with cold water and bring to the boil. Simmer for 3 minutes, then drain and run under cold water until cool. Shell.

3. Roll out one third of the pastry to a 35 x 15 cm (14 x 6 in) rectangle and place it on a baking sheet. Stir the capers, cheese and redcurrants into the rice mixture and spoon half the filling on top of the pastry, leaving a 2.5 cm (1 in) border. Arrange the quail's eggs down the centre of the filling and mound the rest of the rice on top. Brush the edges of the pastry with water.

4. Roll out the remaining pastry to a 43 x 23 cm (17 x 9 in) rectangle and place over the filling. Press the edges together and trim neatly with a knife. Brush with beaten egg and bake for 35 minutes until golden. Serve cut into slices, with Quick Lemon Hollandaise (see page 187).

MINCEMEAT AND CRANBERRY STRUDEL

Serves 6

As you can tell from this book, I use fresh cranberries a lot at Christmas. Their distinctive sour-sweet flavour complements all kinds of dishes both savoury and sweet. In this strudel they balance the richness of the mincemeat.

12 large sheets filo pastry	1 small eating apple, grated
50 g (2 oz) butter, melted	2 tablespoons brandy
350 g (12 oz) vegetarian mincemeat	icing sugar for dusting
175 g (6 oz) fresh cranberries	

1. Preheat the oven to 220°C (425°F, Gas Mark 7). Arrange overlapping sheets of filo in a double layer to form a 45 cm (18 in) square, brushing each sheet with melted butter as you go.

2. Spread the mincemeat over the top half of the pastry, leaving a 5 cm (2 in) border at the top and sides. Scatter over the cranberries, grated apple and brandy. Tuck in the pastry edges, then carefully roll up the strudel.

3. Ease the pastry on to a greased baking sheet and gently curve it into a horseshoe shape. Brush with melted butter and bake for 20–25 minutes until golden. Dust with icing sugar and serve.

MY CHRISTMAS PUDDING

Serves 8

This recipe has slowly evolved over the 20-odd years I've been making Christmas puddings but I think I'm finally there with the definitive version. My family acclaim it as the champion, neither too dark nor too light and with just the right moisture content. I find that butter works well here; not only is it suitable for vegetarians, unlike traditional suet, but it also gives the pudding a lovely flavour and texture.

225 g (8 oz) Lexia raisins	175 g (6 oz) self-raising flour
225 g (8 oz) sultanas	2 teaspoons mixed spice
100 g (4 oz) currants	1 teaspoon freshly grated nutmeg
300 ml (½ pint) Guinness or brown ale	175 g (6 oz) butter
50 g (2 oz) candied peel, chopped	175 g (6 oz) dark muscovado sugar
50 g (2 oz) pine nuts, chopped	3 eggs
50 g (2 oz) blanched almonds, chopped	100 g (4 oz) fresh breadcrumbs
1 eating apple, grated	grated rind and juice of 1 lemon
100 g (4 oz) carrot, grated	4 tablespoons brandy or milk

1. Place the raisins, sultanas and currants in a bowl, pour over the Guinness and leave overnight to soak.

2. The next day, stir the candied peel, pine nuts, almonds, apple and carrot into the soaked fruit. Sift the flour with the spices. Beat the butter with the sugar until fluffy, then beat in the eggs one at a time. Fold in the flour and then stir in the fruit mixture with the breadcrumbs, lemon rind and juice and brandy or milk. Mix thoroughly, then spoon into a greased 1.7 litre (3 pint) pudding basin.

3. Cover the pudding with greaseproof paper and foil, pleated in the centre, and tie securely with string. Steam for 5 hours, topping up the pan regularly with boiling water. Remove the pudding from the pan and leave to cool. Re-cover the pudding with fresh greaseproof and foil and store in a cool dark place for at least a month.

4. To reheat, steam the pudding for a further 3 hours, turn out and serve with brandy butter, cream or custard.

Breads

$\mathcal{M}$AKING YOUR OWN bread can be immensely rewarding, and once you've become familiar with the basic techniques there's no reason why home-made bread shouldn't feature regularly in meals for family and friends. Even the simplest of home-made breads adds cachet to a simple menu and I always find bread-making becomes a talking point when I've served my own loaves.

However, I now tend to make yeasted breads only to serve with uncomplicated menus. Unless I'm blessed with plenty of time (which is rare), if I'm entertaining for large numbers or preparing an elaborate meal I buy some of the excellent breads that are now available in the shops or make up a batch of savoury scones or Irish soda bread. These can be flavoured in all kinds of interesting ways; try the Carrot and Sage Scones on page 182 or Black Olive Soda Bread on page 177.

Caraway Rolls

You can also make the dough for these rolls into a loaf – just shape, place in a 900 g (2 lb) loaf tin and leave until doubled in size, then bake for 25–30 minutes.

450 g (1 lb) strong plain flour	1 teaspoon salt
25 g (1 oz) butter	300 ml (½ pint) milk and water mixed
½ sachet easy-blend yeast	extra caraway seeds for topping
1 tablespoon caraway seeds	

1. Sift the flour into a mixing bowl and rub in the butter. Stir in the yeast, caraway seeds and salt. Warm the water and milk to lukewarm and stir into the flour. Mix to a firm dough, then turn on to a lightly floured work surface and knead for 10 minutes or until smooth and elastic. Place in an oiled bowl and leave in a warm place for an hour or until doubled in size.

2. Preheat the oven to 220°C (425°F, Gas Mark 7). Turn the dough on to a lightly floured surface and knead briefly again. Divide into twelve pieces and shape into rolls or knots. Place on a greased baking sheet, cover with oiled plastic film and leave for 30 minutes or until doubled in size.

3. Brush the rolls with water and sprinkle with caraway seeds. Bake for about 15 minutes or until they are golden on top and sound hollow when tapped underneath. Transfer the rolls to a wire rack to cool.

Black Olive Soda Bread

Makes 1 loaf

Soda bread is very quick to make as it doesn't need to be left to rise – you just mix, shape and bake. It's best eaten fresh but any leftovers can be served toasted and buttered the next day. I make this recipe using a good-quality olive paste but you could just add finely chopped black olives.

680 g (1½ lb) plain flour	40 g (1½ oz) white vegetable fat
1½ teaspoons bicarbonate of soda	150 ml (¼ pint) natural yoghurt
2 teaspoons cream of tartar	150 ml (¼ pint) semi-skimmed milk
1 teaspoon salt	2 tablespoons black olive paste

1. Preheat the oven to 200°C (400°F, Gas Mark 6). Sift the flour, bicarbonate of soda, cream of tartar and salt into a mixing bowl. Rub in the white fat until the mixture resembles fine breadcrumbs. Whisk together the yoghurt and milk and add to the dry ingredients. Mix to a soft dough, stirring in the olive paste as you do so to give a marbled effect.

2. Turn the dough on to a lightly floured work surface and knead lightly and briefly. Shape into a round about 6 cm (2½ in) thick and place on a floured baking sheet. With the handle of a wooden spoon, mark a cross on the top of the loaf about 2 cm (¾ in) deep. Dust the top of the loaf with a little flour.

3. Bake for about 25 minutes until well risen and golden, then transfer to a wire rack to cool. Serve cut into thick slices.

Focaccia with Chilli and Tomato

Makes 1 loaf

For an authentic focaccia it's worth looking out for the flour used in Italy, labelled 00. This gives the loaf its soft-textured crumb and is available in good Italian delicatessens and some supermarkets. It's also useful for making pasta and pizza bases. If you can't get hold of it, strong plain flour will give good results but the bread will have quite a different texture.

450 g (1 lb) Italian 00 flour or strong plain flour	FOR THE TOPPING
1½ teaspoons salt	1 tablespoon sun-dried tomato paste
2 teaspoons easy-blend yeast	1 tablespoon extra virgin olive oil
2 tablespoons olive oil	1 teaspoon chilli oil
	2 teaspoons coarse sea salt

1. Sift the flour and salt together into a mixing bowl and stir in the yeast. Whisk the oil with 300 ml (½ pint) warm water and add to the flour. Mix to form a soft dough, then turn on to a lightly floured work surface and knead for about 10 minutes until smooth and elastic.

2. Place the dough in an oiled plastic bag and leave in a warm place for about 45 minutes or until doubled in size. Meanwhile, whisk together the sun-dried tomato paste, olive oil and chilli oil for the topping.

3. Turn the dough on to a lightly floured surface and knead lightly. Roll out to a rectangle about 25 x 30 cm (10 x 12 in) and transfer to a baking sheet. Mark indentations all over the surface with your thumbs, then cover and leave to rise again for 30 minutes or until doubled in size. Preheat the oven to 220°C (425°F, Gas Mark 7).

4. Gently brush the oil and tomato paste mixture over the dough and sprinkle with the coarse salt. Bake the bread for about 20–25 minutes until golden, then transfer to a wire rack to cool. Serve warm.

Walnut and Chive Loaf

Makes 1 loaf

*I've used Cheshire cheese for this loaf but you could try any strong-flavoured hard cheese.
Serve it with cheese or with soups and starters (see page 15).*

225 g (8 oz) self-raising flour	75 g (3 oz) Cheshire cheese, grated
½ teaspoon mustard powder	4 tablespoons chopped fresh chives
large pinch each of salt and cayenne pepper	1 egg
50 g (2 oz) butter, diced	150 ml (¼ pint) semi-skimmed milk
25 g (1 oz) walnut pieces, finely chopped	extra grated cheese for topping

1. Preheat the oven to 180°C (350°F, Gas Mark 4). Sift the flour into a mixing bowl with the mustard, salt and cayenne. Rub in the butter until the mixture resembles fine breadcrumbs, then stir in the walnuts, cheese and chives.

2. Beat together the egg and milk and stir into the dry ingredients. Mix well, then spoon into a greased and base-lined 450 g (1 lb) loaf tin. Level the surface, sprinkle with cheese and bake for 40–45 minutes until golden and firm to the touch. Turn on to a wire rack to cool and serve sliced and buttered.

ROSEMARY, LEMON AND GARLIC PIZZA BREAD

Serves 4

I love the garlic bread served in good pizzerias – basically it's just pizza dough rolled out thinly and brushed with garlic butter. Less indigestible than the more common version made with a French stick, it's very easy to prepare at home. I like to vary the flavourings, and this recipe adds lemon and rosemary to the garlic.

225 g (8 oz) strong plain flour	FOR THE TOPPING
1 teaspoon salt	50 g (2 oz) softened butter
½ sachet easy-blend yeast	1 tablespoon chopped fresh rosemary
1 tablespoon olive oil	2 garlic cloves, finely chopped
	1 teaspoon grated lemon rind
	salt and freshly ground black pepper

1. Sift the flour and salt into a mixing bowl and stir in the yeast. Mix the oil with 150 ml (¼ pint) warm water and add to the dry ingredients. Mix to a soft dough, then turn on to a lightly floured work surface and knead for 8–10 minutes until smooth and elastic. Place in an oiled plastic bag and leave in a warm place for about 45 minutes or until doubled in size.

2. Preheat the oven to 220°C (425°F, Gas Mark 7). Turn the dough on to a work surface and knead lightly. Divide in two and roll each piece into a circle about 5 mm (¼ in) thick. Place on baking sheets and slash the top of each circle about five times with a sharp knife. Bake for 12–15 minutes until golden and crisp.

3. While the dough is cooking beat together all the ingredients for the topping. As soon as the pizzas come out of the oven, spread them with the flavoured butter. Cut into strips and serve immediately.

Red Onion and Pine Nut Focaccia Rolls

Makes 4

This recipe is based on a focaccia dough and made into individual flat rolls (see pages 122-23). Slice them in half and fill with Roasted Peppers with Mozzarella (see page 30) for the world's greatest sandwich. To make Rosemary Focaccia Rolls, omit the onions and pine nuts from the topping and sprinkle with coarse salt and olive oil.

350 g (12 oz) Italian 00 flour (see page 178) or strong plain flour	*FOR THE TOPPING*
	1 medium red onion, sliced
1 teaspoon salt	*2 tablespoons pine nuts*
1 tablespoon chopped fresh rosemary	*1 teaspoon coarse sea salt*
2 teaspoons easy-blend yeast	*2 tablespoons extra virgin olive oil*
1 tablespoon olive oil	

1. Make the dough following the instructions for Focaccia with Chilli and Tomato (see page 178), adding the rosemary to the flour and using about 200 ml (7 fl oz) warm water to mix. Knead and leave to double in size as instructed.

2. Lightly knead the risen dough again and divide it into four. Roll each piece into a rectangle about 1 cm (½ in) thick and place on a baking sheet. Dimple the surface of the dough with your thumbs, cover and leave to rise again for 30 minutes or until doubled in size. Preheat the oven to 200°C (400°F, Gas Mark 6).

3. Scatter the onion, pine nuts and salt over the focaccia and drizzle with the olive oil. Bake for about 15 minutes until puffy and golden. Leave to cool on a wire rack and serve warm.

CARROT AND SAGE SCONES

*I like to make these savoury scones very small and serve them split and topped with
mascarpone or other soft cheeses for nibbles. They are also good for
packed lunches and picnics or with soups.*

225 g (8 oz) self-raising flour	1 tablespoon chopped fresh sage
1 teaspoon salt	1 medium carrot, finely grated
½ teaspoon baking powder	150 ml (¼ pint) natural yoghurt
25 g (1 oz) butter	a little milk to glaze

1. Preheat the oven to 200°C (400°F, Gas Mark 6). Sift the flour, salt and baking powder into a bowl and rub in the butter until the mixture resembles breadcrumbs. Stir in the sage and carrot, then add the yoghurt and mix to a soft dough.

2. Turn the dough on to a lightly floured work surface and knead lightly. Roll out until 1 cm (½ in) thick and cut into 2.5 cm (1 in) rounds with a plain cutter. Re-roll the trimmings and cut more scones. Place on a floured baking sheet and brush the tops with milk.

3. Bake for 12–15 minutes until well risen and golden. Transfer to a wire rack to cool.

Sauces

Well-flavoured sauces can make all the difference to a meal; used skilfully, they add a burst of concentrated flavour that should enhance, but not overpower, the main elements in a dish. Always select really fresh, high-quality ingredients for sauces to give them the maximum impact, and taste to ensure the correct amount of seasoning, bearing in mind the flavourings of the dish you plan to serve the sauce with.

The recipes in this chapter are all ones that I use over and over again. I've included a good savoury gravy, quick hollandaise sauce and a spicy salsa plus that essential – a tasty vegetable stock. All have many uses, and Spicy Peanut Sauce, Tomato and Chilli Salsa and Roasted Aubergine Mayonnaise also double up as dips.

Tomato and Chilli Salsa

Serves 4–6

This uncooked sauce should only be made when tomatoes are at their best. Serve it with vegetable fritters or Herbed Drop Scones (see page 22), or as a relish with all kinds of salads.

450 g (1 lb) ripe tomatoes, finely chopped	1 red chilli, seeded and finely chopped
4 spring onions, finely chopped	4–6 tablespoons extra virgin olive oil
3 tablespoons chopped fresh basil	salt and freshly ground black pepper
2 tablespoons chopped fresh mint	

1. Place all the ingredients except the seasoning in a small bowl and mix well. Leave to stand at room temperature for at least 2 hours, stirring occasionally, then season to taste and serve.

Onion Gravy

Makes 600 ml (1 pint)

Make this gravy with a well-flavoured vegetable stock and be sure not to let the onion burn or it will ruin the flavour.

2 large onions, sliced	½ teaspoon tomato purée
1 tablespoon olive oil	1 teaspoon red wine vinegar or balsamic vinegar
2 tablespoons plain flour	1 teaspoon chopped fresh thyme
600 ml (1 pint) vegetable stock (see page 186)	salt and freshly ground black pepper

1. Put the onions in a frying pan with the oil and cook gently for 15 minutes, stirring occasionally, until softened but not coloured. Raise the heat, sprinkle with a little salt and cook for a further 5 minutes until golden.

2. Stir in the flour and cook for 1 minute, then gradually add the stock, tomato purée, vinegar and thyme. Bring to the boil, stirring, and simmer for 3 minutes. Season to taste and serve. Purée the gravy in a blender if you prefer a smooth sauce.

Caribbean Rice & Peas
Paella
Vegetable Curry
Sausage Casserole
Cold Weather Casserole
Provençal bean stew.
Winter couscous.
Chilli!
Italian veg stew.
Mushroom stroganoff.

SPICY PEANUT SAUCE

Serves 4

This quick sauce can be served as a dip, with vegetable saté, or tossed into stir fries.
Thin it down with extra coconut milk if you want to serve it over vegetables.

1 teaspoon sunflower oil	1 teaspoon dark muscovado sugar
1 garlic clove, crushed	1 tablespoon lemon juice
4 tablespoons crunchy peanut butter	½ teaspoon chilli paste
1 tablespoon dark soy sauce	4 tablespoons canned coconut milk

1. Heat the oil in a small pan, add the garlic and cook over a medium heat for
1 minute until golden. Add the peanut butter and 4 tablespoons cold water and mix
well.

2. Remove from the heat and stir in the soy sauce, sugar, lemon juice and chilli
paste. Return the pan to the heat and cook gently, stirring, until the sauce is smooth.
Stir in the coconut milk, heat through and serve. Store in a screw-topped jar in the
fridge for up to a week.

CUMBERLAND SAUCE

Serves 4

This sauce is traditionally served with ham but I serve it with roasted vegetables, as an
accompaniment to Pine Nut and Pepper Terrine (see page 168), with rice or potato dishes
or with baked stuffed onions.

1 lemon	100 g (4 oz) good-quality redcurrant jelly
1 orange	1 teaspoon Dijon mustard
1 tablespoon sunflower oil	2 tablespoons port
1 shallot, finely chopped	salt and freshly ground black pepper

1. Pare the rind from the lemon and orange with a vegetable peeler and cut it into thin shreds. Place in a bowl, cover with boiling water and leave to stand for 1 minute. Drain the shreds and set aside. Squeeze the juice from the lemon and orange.

2. Heat the oil in a small pan and cook the shallot over a medium heat for 3 minutes until softened. Stir in the redcurrant jelly, mustard, orange and lemon juice and stir over a gentle heat until the jelly melts and the sauce is smooth. Bring to the boil and simmer gently for 5 minutes. Stir in the port, season to taste and serve.

ROASTED AUBERGINE MAYONNAISE

Serves 4–6

Roasting aubergines gives them a wonderfully rich, smoky flavour, making this mayonnaise an excellent sauce or dip (see page 23).

1 large aubergine	1 dried chilli, seeded and chopped
1 egg yolk	juice of ½ lemon
2 garlic cloves, crushed	½ teaspoon sesame oil
150 ml (¼ pint) olive oil	salt and freshly ground black pepper

1. Preheat the oven to 220°C (425°F, Gas Mark 7). Place the aubergine in a roasting tin and bake for 30 minutes until the skin is blackened and the flesh tender. Leave to cool and then peel off the skin. Purée the flesh in a blender or food processor until smooth.

2. Place the egg yolk in a bowl with the garlic and the aubergine purée and beat well to combine. Drip in the oil a little at a time, beating constantly as the mixture thickens. Stir in the chilli, lemon juice, sesame oil and seasoning. Chill until ready to serve.

VEGETABLE STOCK

Makes 600 ml (1 pint)

A good stock forms the base of many dishes and is particularly important in vegetarian cooking. Stock freezes well, so make up a large batch, simmer until well reduced and freeze it in ice trays to provide convenient, quickly defrosted quantities for future use.

1 onion, quartered	6 black peppercorns
1 celery stick, quartered	1 bay leaf
4 carrots, halved	3 sprigs of fresh parsley
100 g (4 oz) flat mushrooms (optional)	sprig of fresh thyme

1. Preheat the oven to 220°C (425°F, Gas Mark 7). Place the vegetables in a roasting tin and roast in the oven for 45 minutes until golden but not burnt. Add 900 ml (1½ pints) cold water and stir, scraping off any vegetables stuck to the tin.

2. Transfer the contents of the tin to a large saucepan and add the peppercorns and herbs. Bring to the boil and simmer for 1 hour, then strain and leave to cool. Chill until required.

QUICK LEMON HOLLANDAISE

Serves 4–6

This cheat's hollandaise is ideal when you're entertaining and don't want to spend hours away from your guests. It does need to be made in a blender, however – a food processor is no good. Have all the ingredients ready in advance and you can whizz it up in an instant. Serve with steamed vegetables – classically asparagus and artichokes – or with any of the pastry dishes in this book (see page 71).

3 tablespoons white wine vinegar	3 egg yolks
2 teaspoons chopped fresh tarragon	100 g (4 oz) unsalted butter
6 black peppercorns	grated rind and juice of ½ lemon
1 shallot, finely chopped	salt and freshly ground black pepper

1. Place the vinegar in a small pan with the tarragon, peppercorns and shallot. Bring to the boil and cook until the vinegar is reduced to 1 tablespoon. Strain and leave to cool.

2. Place the reduced vinegar in the goblet of a blender with the egg yolks and process briefly to mix. Heat the butter in a small pan until bubbling but not browned. With the blender running, pour the butter on to the egg yolks in a steady stream. The sauce should be thick and creamy. Stir in the lemon rind and juice, season to taste and serve immediately.

Fresh Tomato Sauce

Makes about 450 ml (¾ pint)

I only bother making this in middle or late summer when the tomatoes are sufficiently flavoursome, otherwise I use tinned Italian plum tomatoes. However, the fresh sauce freezes well so if you have time it is worth making up a large batch and freezing it. If you want a coarser-textured sauce, skin and deseed the tomatoes before cooking and don't sieve it. Other flavourings such as chopped chillies or garlic can be added with the basil, but if the tomatoes are really good you shouldn't need anything else.

2 tablespoons olive oil	680 g (1½ lb) fresh ripe tomatoes, chopped
4 tablespoons chopped fresh basil	salt and freshly ground black pepper

1. Heat the oil in a medium pan until very hot, add the basil and cook for 30 seconds. Stir in the tomatoes and seasoning. Bring to the boil and simmer, stirring occasionally, for 20–25 minutes, until the sauce is thick and pulpy.

2. Sieve to remove the skins and seeds, then return the sauce to a clean pan and heat through. Check the seasoning and serve hot or cold.

Pesto Sauce

Makes about 150 ml (¼ pint)

This simple Italian sauce has become enormously popular in recent years. It is invaluable for all kinds of dishes, as its distinctive flavour adds a welcome punch to pasta, soups and vegetables. Though the bottled versions on sale are much better than they used to be they still don't match the real thing made with fresh basil. If you grow your own basil, which is a good idea if you want to make pesto regularly, try the small-leaf variety, which has the best flavour. Pesto freezes well but should be frozen before you add the Parmesan; I freeze it in ice-cube trays for maximum convenience.

75 g (3 oz) fresh basil leaves	100 ml (3½ fl oz) extra virgin olive oil
25 g (1 oz) pine nuts	25 g (1 oz) freshly grated Parmesan cheese
2 garlic cloves, peeled	salt and freshly ground black pepper

1. Place the basil, pine nuts, garlic and olive oil in a blender or food processor and process on high speed until the ingredients are fairly smooth and well blended. Stop at intervals to push the ingredients down with a spatula.

2. Transfer the paste to a bowl and beat in the Parmesan, then season to taste. Store in a covered container in the fridge for up to a week. If using with pasta, stir a couple of tablespoons of the pasta cooking water into the pesto to thin it down before adding to the pasta.

OLIVE OIL DRESSING

Makes about 150 ml (¼ pint)

A good dressing is essential for salads and one of the simplest sauces to make. Despite this, people often seem to have problems with it, and I think the most common fault is to use too much vinegar. This is my standard recipe but I recommend always tasting as you mix to ensure the balance of acidity suits you. Sometimes I add a dash of balsamic vinegar for extra flavour but you should be able to make a good dressing without it. I always use my best extra virgin olive oil, however, and make sure that the salad leaves are lightly coated, not drenched in oil. Always dress a green salad just before serving it.

2–3 tablespoons white wine vinegar or fresh lemon juice	*salt and freshly ground black pepper*
1 teaspoon Dijon mustard	*crushed garlic, chopped fresh herbs, grated lemon rind for flavouring (optional)*
125 ml (4 fl oz) olive oil (about 8 tablespoons)	

1. Place the vinegar, mustard and seasoning in a screw-topped jar and shake until well blended. Add the oil and shake again until emulsified. Taste and add more oil or vinegar as necessary (I sometimes dip a salad leaf in at this stage to check the balance of flavours).

2. Add any of the optional flavourings. Store in the fridge for up to a week.

Menu Suggestions

A Formal Winter Dinner
Double-gingered Tomato Broth (page 16)

∽

Wild Mushroom and Leek Croustades (page 73)
*Honey- and Mustard-roasted New Potatoes
and Shallots (page 124)*
French Beans with Roasted Almonds (page 120)

∽

*Warm Chocolate Cake with
Cinnamon Mascarpone (page 142)*

Christmas Dinner
*Stilton and Apple Soup with Walnut Cream
(page 18)*

∽

*Quail's Egg, Saffron and Wild Rice Filo Wreath
(page 169)*
Creamy Celeriac and Sprout Purée (page 171)
Spinach with Raisins and Pine Nuts (page 126)

∽

My Christmas Pudding (page 174)
Brandy Ice Cream (page 150)

A Summer Barbecue
*Herbed Soft Cheese with Green Peppercorns
(page 32)*

∽

A Vegetable Barbecue (page 98)
*New Potato Salad with Tarragon and Orange
(page 121)*
Fresh Beetroot Salad with Caraway (page 127)
*Red Onion and Pine Nut Focaccia Rolls
(page 181)*

∽

Fresh Raspberry Tart (page 146)

A Casual Supper Any Time
Bruschetta with Parsley and Red Onion (page 33)

∽

Roasted Aubergine and Olive Lasagne (page 42)
Warm Courgette Salad (page 120)
Focaccia with Chilli and Tomato (page 178)

∽

Baked Figs with Orange (page 134)

An Autumn Supper Party
*Double-cooked Goat's Cheese and
Watercress Soufflés (page 27)*

∽

Golden Vegetable and Bean Stew (page 106)
*Black Olive Soda Bread (page 177) and salad of
your choice*

∽

Poached Pears in Ginger Wine (page 141)

A Family Sunday Lunch
Curried Pumpkin Soup (page 14)

∽

Hazelnut, Leek and Mushroom Terrine (page 90)
*Roasted Root Vegetables with Cranberry
Orange Sauce (page 85)*
Leek and Onion Yorkshire Pudding (page 93)
Onion Gravy (page 184)

∽

Apricot Toffee Pudding (page 136)

A Celebration Party For 12
Herbed Drop Scones (page 22)
Mushroom and Garlic Crostini (page 25)

∽

Roasted Vegetable Terrine (page 96)
Onion Tart with Black Olive Pastry (page 74)
*Marinated Mushroom Salad with
Sesame Dressing (page 119)*
Chick Pea and Tomato Salad (page 105)
*Leafy Salad with Croutons and Pine Nut Dressing
(page 125)*

∽

*Hazelnut Roulade with Raspberries
and Redcurrants (page 149)*
Amaretti and Chocolate Cake (page 147)

A Teenagers' Party For 12
Vegetable Samosas (page 160)

∽

Red Bean and Potato Chilli (page 109)
Roasted Peppers with Mozzarella (page 30)
Mixed leaf salad (no recipe)
*Rosemary, Lemon and Garlic Pizza Bread
(page 180)*

∽

Apricot and Ginger Crumble (page 133)

Index